Job Satisfaction

Application,
Assessment,
Cause, and
Consequences

Paul E. Spector

Advanced Topics in
Organizational Behavior ATOB

SAGE Publications
International Educational and Professional Publisher
Thousand Oaks   London   New Delhi

For information, address to:

SAGE Publications, Inc.
2455 Teller Road
Thousand Oaks, California 91320
E-mail: order@sagepub.com

SAGE Publications Ltd.
6 Bonhill Street
London EC2A 4PU
United Kingdom

SAGE Publications India Pvt. Ltd.
M-32 Market
Greater Kailash I
New Delhi 110 048 India

Printed in the United States of America

Library of Congress Cataloging-in-Publication Data

Spector, Paul E.
    Job satisfaction: Application, assessment, causes, and
consequences / author, Paul E. Spector.
        p.   cm. — (Advanced topics in organizational behavior)
    Includes bibliographical references and index.
    ISBN 0-7619-8922-6 (acid-free paper). — ISBN 0-7619-8923-4 (pbk.
: acid-free paper)
        1. Job satisfaction.   I. Title.   II. Series.
    HF5549.5.J63S635   1997
    158.7–dc21   97-4598

97 98 99 00 01 02 03   10 9 8 7 6 5 4 3 2 1

Acquiring Editor:	Marquita Flemming
Editorial Assistant:	Frances Borghi
Production Editor:	Astrid Virding
Production Assistant:	Denise Santoyo
Typesetter/Designer:	Yang-hee Syn Maresca
Print Buyer:	Anna Chin

Contents

Preface

J ob satisfaction is the degree to which people like their jobs. Some people enjoy work and find it to be a central part of life. Others hate to work and do so only because they must. The study of the causes and consequences of these important employee attitudes is one of the major domains of industrial-organizational psychology and organizational behavior. More studies have been done to understand job satisfaction than for any other variable in organizations. In addition, the assessment of employee attitudes such as job satisfaction has become a common activity in organizations in which management is concerned with the physical and psychological well-being of people.

This book will provide an overview of the vast job satisfaction research literature. It covers the assessment, causes, consequences, and nature of this important variable. Although the primary focus is on the findings and theories from the organizational behavior literature, we will also pay some attention to applications conducted within organizations to improve efficiency and the quality of working life. Job satisfaction is associated with many important behaviors and outcomes for employees that have implications for organizational and personal well-being.

This book is intended to be an introduction to the field of job satisfaction. By necessity, it provides only an overview of the major issues and research findings, for a detailed treatment of this topic would require several volumes. The reader is assumed to have some background in industrial-organizational psychology or organizational behavior. Some familiarity with basic research methodology would be helpful. Although the book is not particularly technical, there are a few statistical terms used, such as the *correlation coefficient.*

This book is organized into six chapters. Chapter 1 discusses the nature of job satisfaction, including what it is and why it is an important topic for concern in organizations. The assessment of job satisfaction is the topic of Chapter 2. Both the development of new scales and use of existing scales are covered. Chapter 3 focuses on how people feel about work. Included will be findings on job satisfaction differences for various demographic groups, as well as cross-country comparisons. Job satisfaction causes are covered in Chapter 4, including both organizational environment and personal factors. Potential effects of job satisfaction on employees and thereby on their organizations are discussed in Chapter 5. Potential effects range from the physical and psychological well-being of employees to job performance and withdrawal. Finally, Chapter 6 mentions how organizations might measure job satisfaction and respond constructively to employee concerns.

No one writes a book such as this one without the assistance of others. I would like to thank Steve M. Jex and the series editors Julian Barling and Kevin Kelloway for their helpful comments and suggestions on the initial draft of this book.

1

The Nature of
Job Satisfaction

Every year, IBM conducts opinion surveys to find out among other things how employees feel about their jobs. Managers at IBM are very concerned about the job satisfaction of employees. It is seen as one factor that is important for business effectiveness. The high level of employee job satisfaction at IBM contributes to low employee turnover and the outstanding company reputation. IBM is seen as a good employer, which helps it attract high-quality job applicants to fill its positions.

Job satisfaction is a topic of wide interest to both people who work in organizations and people who study them. In fact, it is the most frequently studied variable in organizational behavior research. It is a central variable in both research and theory of organizational phenomena ranging from job design to supervision. Literally thousands of job satisfaction studies can be found in the journals of organizational behavior and related fields.

There are important reasons why we should be concerned with job satisfaction, which can be classified according to the focus on the employee or the organization. First, the humanitarian perspective is that people deserve to be treated fairly and with respect. Job satisfaction is to some extent a reflection of good treatment. It also can be considered an indicator of emotional well-being or psychological health. Second, the utilitarian perspective is that job satisfaction can lead to behavior by employees that affects organizational functioning. As we will see later in this book, there are important implications of employee feelings, which can lead to both positive and negative behaviors. Furthermore, job satisfaction can be a reflection of organizational functioning. Differences among organizational units in job satisfaction can be diagnostic of potential trouble spots. Each reason is sufficient to justify concern with job satisfaction. Combined they explain and justify the attention that is paid to this important variable.

Managers in many organizations, such as IBM, share the concerns of researchers for the job satisfaction of employees. The assessment of job satisfaction is a common activity in many organizations where management feels that employee well-being is important. The motives can be for humanitarian and/or pragmatic reasons, but employee job satisfaction is an important goal. In the rest of this book, we will discuss factors that influence job satisfaction and ramifications of this variable for employees and organizations.

What Is Job Satisfaction?

Job satisfaction is simply how people feel about their jobs and different aspects of their jobs. It is the extent to which people like (satisfaction) or dislike (dissatisfaction) their jobs. As it is generally assessed, job satisfaction is an attitudinal variable. In the past, job satisfaction was approached by some researchers from the perspective of need fulfillment—that is, whether or not the job met the employee's physical and psychological needs for the things provided by work, such as pay (e.g., Porter, 1962; Wolf, 1970). However, this approach has been de-emphasized because today most researchers tend to focus attention on cognitive processes rather than on underlying needs. The attitudinal perspective has become the predominant one in the study of job satisfaction.

Job satisfaction can be considered as a global feeling about the job or as a related constellation of attitudes about various aspects or facets of the job. The global approach is used when the overall or bottom line attitude is of interest, for example, if one wishes to determine the effects of people liking or disliking their

TABLE 1.1 Common Job Satisfaction Facets

Appreciation
Communication
Coworkers
Fringe benefits
Job conditions
Nature of the work itself
Organization itself
Organization's policies and procedures
Pay
Personal growth
Promotion opportunities
Recognition
Security
Supervision

---

jobs. Most of the research we will discuss assessed global job satisfaction in relation to other variables of interest. The facet approach is used to find out which parts of the job produce satisfaction or dissatisfaction. This can be very useful for organizations that wish to identify areas of dissatisfaction that they can improve. Sometimes both approaches can be used to get a complete picture of employee job satisfaction.

A job satisfaction facet can be concerned with any aspect or part of a job. Facets frequently assessed include rewards such as pay or fringe benefits, other people such as coworkers or supervisors, the nature of the work itself, and the organization itself. Table 1.1 contains facets that can be found in some of the most popular job satisfaction instruments, which will be discussed in the next chapter. Sometimes organizations will be interested in very specific facets not found in an existing scale, such as satisfaction with particular policies or practices unique to that organization.

The facet approach can provide a more complete picture of a person's job satisfaction than the global approach. An employee can have very different feelings about the various facets. He or she might like coworkers and dislike pay, a common pattern for Americans. As we will see in Chapter 3, however, patterns can be different in other countries.

Not only do people differ in their satisfaction across facets, but the facets are only modestly related to one another. Table 1.2 contains intercorrelations among

TABLE 1.2 Intercorrelations Among JSS Subscales

	1	2	3	4	5	6	7	8
1 Pay								
2 Promotion	.53							
3 Supervision	.19	.25						
4 Benefits	.45	.36	.10					
5 Contingent rewards	.54	.58	.46	.38				
6 Operating procedures	.31	.31	.17	.29	.46			
7 Coworkers	.19	.23	.42	.16	.39	.22		
8 Nature of work	.25	.32	.31	.20	.47	.30	.32	
9 Communication	.40	.45	.39	.30	.59	.44	.42	.43

SOURCE: Spector (1985).
NOTE: $n = 3027$. All correlations are significant at $p < .001$.

the nine facets of the Job Satisfaction Survey or JSS (Spector, 1985), which is one of the many existing scales. As can be seen, the correlations among the facets tend to be rather small. This pattern of results is convincing evidence that people have distinctly different feelings about the various facets of the job. They tend not to have global feelings that produce the same level of satisfaction with every job aspect.

There has been a lot of work conducted to determine the underlying structure of job satisfaction facets. Most studies have used complex statistics (e.g., factor analysis) to reduce people's responses to a large number of facets to a smaller number of underlying dimensions of job satisfaction. These studies, summarized by Locke (1976), have suggested several structures. They clearly separate facets into the four areas noted earlier: rewards, other people, nature of the work, and organizational context. The intercorrelations among the facets in Table 1.2 are consistent with this structure in that facets correlate more strongly with other facets in their area than facets not in their area. For example, the reward facets of fringe benefits and pay correlate more strongly with one another than with the organizational context facets of communication or operating procedures.

2

The Assessment of Job Satisfaction

J ob satisfaction is usually measured with interviews or questionnaires administered to the job incumbents in question. Although interviews are used in some cases, most research is done with questionnaires. This is because interviews are expensive and time consuming to conduct. By contrast, one can survey a large number of people with a paper-and-pencil questionnaire with very little effort or expense. Furthermore, it is easy to quantify and standardize questionnaire responses. However, it is possible to get more extensive information in an interview, as respondents can elaborate about the issues that they are discussing. In addition, the less constrained format of an interview allows for the emergence of points that are not preplanned by the researcher. The respondents can generate their own areas of satisfaction or dissatisfaction. This is particularly helpful as an initial step in designing a questionnaire, for items can be written to tap those areas uncovered during interviews.

There have been a few attempts to use alternative procedures to assess job satisfaction. Spector, Dwyer, and Jex (1988) asked supervisors to estimate the job satisfaction of their subordinates. The correlation was .54 between incumbents and supervisors, suggesting that the supervisors may have been very aware of the feelings toward the job held by their subordinates. Glick, Jenkins, and Gupta (1986) had observers estimate people's job satisfaction after watching them work for about 2 hours. Again, there was moderate agreement between the two sources. There has even been a study where elementary school children were asked to estimate the satisfaction of their parents (Trice & Tillapaugh, 1991) and a study in which husbands were asked about their wives' satisfaction with being working mothers (Barling & MacEwen, 1988). In both studies, there was reasonable agreement between incumbents and the other sources of job satisfaction information. Of course, in no case is the agreement high enough to conclude that the alternative sources are equivalent to asking the individuals directly about their job satisfaction.

Perhaps the easiest way to assess job satisfaction is to use one of the existing scales. Several have been carefully developed, and in many studies, their reliability and validity have been established. Reliability refers to consistency in measurement: That is, if we repeatedly assess the job satisfaction of a person will we get the same number each time, assuming the person's attitudes do not change? Validity concerns our interpretation of what a scale actually assesses: That is, does our job satisfaction scale assess people's feelings concerning their jobs? It is not necessarily the case that a scale is reliable, as items can be confusing and lead to inconsistent responses by people. Furthermore, some scales might not assess what we intend to measure. If employees are concerned about supervisors' seeing their responses to sensitive questions, they might not be honest on a questionnaire. Thus, responses will not reflect true feelings.

There are many advantages to using an existing job satisfaction scale. First, many of the available scales cover the major facets of satisfaction. Often, these facets are those of interest in a satisfaction survey. Second, most existing scales have been used a sufficient number of times to provide norms, which are the means on each facet for people in general within a given population, such as all private sector managers in the United States. Comparisons with norms can help with the interpretation of results from a given organization.

Third, many existing scales have been shown to exhibit acceptable levels of reliability. Fourth, their use in research provides good evidence for construct validity. Thus, one can have confidence that the scale will consistently measure the satisfaction facets of interest. Finally, the use of an existing scale saves the considerable cost and time necessary to develop a scale from scratch.

The major disadvantage of using an existing scale is that it will be limited to only those facets that the developers chose to place in their instrument. The facets of most scales tend to be general, which makes them applicable to most organizations. They will not include more specific areas of satisfaction or dissatisfaction that are issues for certain types of organizations or a particular organization. These could include satisfaction with specific decisions, events, individuals, or policies. One might assess, for example, satisfaction with the particular health insurance company that is used or with the policy for rewarding people who are not absent from work. In a hospital, one might wish to determine satisfaction with how employees are assigned to shifts, or with the quality assurance procedures.

The cost of using an existing job satisfaction scale can sometimes be prohibitive, especially if large numbers of employees are to be surveyed. Many scales are copyrighted and authors might charge a fee for their use. For example, the current price for copies of the Job Descriptive Index, one of the most popular scales (see p. 12 for a detailed description) is $47 per hundred, including shipping and handling fees. The current book includes a copy and description of the Job Satisfaction Survey (JSS; Spector, 1985), which can be used and modified without fee only for noncommercial educational and research purposes.

This chapter will describe six job satisfaction scales, four facet scales, and two global satisfaction scales. The JSS, the Job Descriptive Index (JDI; Smith, Kendall, & Hulin, 1969), the Minnesota Satisfaction Questionnaire (MSQ; Weiss, Dawis, England, & Lofquist, 1967), and the Job Diagnostic Survey (JDS; Hackman & Oldham, 1975) are facet measures of job satisfaction. Each has been used in many research studies. The JDI has been the most popular with researchers. The two general job satisfaction scales are the Job in General Scale (JIG; Ironson, Smith, Brannick, Gibson, & Paul, 1989), and the Michigan Organizational Assessment Questionnaire satisfaction subscale (Cammann, Fichman, Jenkins, & Klesh, 1979).

Many other job satisfaction scales have been developed besides the six discussed here. Perhaps the best single source of information about other scales is Cook, Hepworth, Wall, and Warr's (1981) book on organizational instruments. Many consulting firms have their own scales that they use when hired to conduct surveys. The Gallup Organization will conduct such surveys, for example, using their own or custom-made scales. We will discuss the development of scales after we discuss six existing scales.

TABLE 2.1 Facets From the Job Satisfaction Survey

Facet	Description
Pay	Satisfaction with pay and pay raises
Promotion	Satisfaction with promotion opportunities
Supervision	Satisfaction with the person's immediate supervisor
Fringe benefits	Satisfaction with fringe benefits
Contingent rewards	Satisfaction with rewards (not necessarily monetary) given for good performance
Operating conditions	Satisfaction with rules and procedures
Coworkers	Satisfaction with coworkers
Nature of Work	Satisfaction with the type of work done
Communication	Satisfaction with communication within the organization

The Job Satisfaction Survey (JSS)

The Job Satisfaction Survey (JSS; Spector, 1985) assesses nine facets of job satisfaction, as well as overall satisfaction. Table 2.1 lists the nine facets, along with a brief description of each. The scale contains 36 items and uses a summated rating scale format. This format is the most popular for job satisfaction scales. The format of the JSS makes it relatively easy to modify. Each of the nine facet subscales contain four items, and a total satisfaction score can be computed by combining all of the items.

A copy of the scale itself is in the Appendix. Each of the items is a statement that is either favorable or unfavorable about an aspect of the job. The first item, for example, concerns pay, and the second concerns promotion opportunities. Respondents are asked to circle one of six numbers that corresponds to their agreement or disagreement about each item.

Scoring of the Job Satisfaction Survey

The JSS can yield 10 scores. Each of the nine subscales can produce a separate facet score. The total of all items produces a total score. Each of the nine JSS subscales is scored by combining responses to its four items. Table 2.2 indicates which items go into each subscale. It also indicates which items need to be reverse scored, as will be explained later.

TABLE 2.2 Subscale Contents for the Job Satisfaction Survey

Subscale	Item Number
Pay	1, 10r, 19r, 28
Promotion	2r, 11, 20, 33
Supervision	3, 12r, 21r, 30
Fringe benefits	4r, 13, 22, 29r
Contingent rewards	5, 14r, 23r, 32r
Operating conditions	6r, 15, 24r, 31r
Coworkers	7, 16r, 25, 34r
Nature of work	8r, 17, 27, 35
Communication	9, 18r, 26r, 36r

NOTE: Items followed by "r" should be reverse-scored.

To compute the various scores, responses to the individual items need to be summed together. As can be seen in the Appendix, the responses to the JSS items are numbered from 1 to 6. A respondent, therefore, can have a score from 1 to 6 for each item. However, some of the items are scored in a positive and some in a negative direction. A positively worded item is one for which agreement indicates job satisfaction. The first item in the scale, "I feel I am being paid a fair amount for the work I do," is positively worded. A negatively worded item is one for which agreement indicates dissatisfaction. Item number 10, "Raises are too few and far between," is negatively worded. Before the items are combined, the scoring for the negatively worded items must be reversed. Thus, people who agree with positively worded items and disagree with negatively worded items will have high scores representing satisfaction. People who disagree with positively worded items and agree with negatively worded items will have low scores representing dissatisfaction. Without item reversals, most respondents will have middle scores because they will tend to agree with half and disagree with half of the items, just because they are worded in opposite directions.

To reverse the scoring you renumber the negatively worded item responses from 6 to 1 rather than 1 to 6. The response "Disagree very much" becomes a 6 rather than a 1. The response "Agree very much" becomes a 1 rather than a 6. Likewise, "Disagree moderately" becomes a 5 rather than a 2 and "Agree moderately" becomes a 2 rather than a 5, and "Disagree slightly" is scored 4 rather than 3, and "Agree slightly" is scored 3 rather than 4. An easy way to reverse-score an item is to subtract respondent scores on the item from the sum of the lowest and

TABLE 2.3 Internal Consistency Reliability for the Job Satisfaction Survey

Subscale	Coefficient Alpha	Test-Retest Reliability
Pay	.75	.45
Promotion	.73	.62
Supervision	.82	.55
Benefits	.73	.37
Contingent rewards	.76	.59
Operating procedures	.62	.74
Coworkers	.60	.64
Nature of work	.78	.54
Communication	.71	.65
Total	.91	.71
Sample size	2,870	43

NOTE: Test-retest reliability was assessed over an 18-month time span.

highest possible responses. For example, with the JSS subtract each item from the sum of 1 and 6, or 7. This can easily be done with the standard statistical packages, such as the SAS System or SPSSX. In the SAS System, to reverse-score an item of the JSS, use the following statement: ITEM2 = 7–ITEM2.

After the items are reversed, the numbered responses for the appropriate items are summed. The total satisfaction score is the sum of all 36 items. Individual facet scores are computed by summing the appropriate items, as shown in Table 2.2. Because each item's score can range from 1 to 6, the individual facet scores can range from 4 to 24. This is because each facet has four items, so the lowest score is the sum of four ones, and the highest score is the sum of four sixes. The total score can range from 36 to 216.

Reliability, Validity, and Norms for the JSS

Reliability

Two types of reliability estimates are important for evaluating a scale. First, internal consistency reliability estimates refer to how well items of a scale relate to one another. High internal consistency reflects the assessment of the same underlying variable. Table 2.3 shows internal consistencies, or coefficient alphas, from a sample of 3,067 individuals who completed the JSS. These coefficient alphas ranged from .60 for the coworker subscale, to .91 for the total scale. The widely accepted minimum standard for internal consistency is .70 (Nunnally, 1978), meaning that the coworker subscale is somewhat lower than researchers like to see.

Second, test-retest reliability reflects the stability of the scale over time. Reliability data are available for the JSS from only one small sample of 43 employees. These reliabilities, shown in Table 2.3, ranged from .37 to .74. The relative stability of satisfaction is remarkable in that the time span was 18 months during which several major changes occurred. These included a reorganization, layoffs, and a change of top administration. The stability of job satisfaction over time will be discussed further in Chapter 4 when we cover dispositional causes of job attitudes.

Validity

Validity evidence for job satisfaction scales is provided by studies that compared different scales with one another on the same employees. For example, five of the JSS subscales (pay, promotion, supervision, coworkers, and nature of work) correlate well with corresponding subscales of the JDI (Smith et al., 1969), which is probably the most carefully validated scale of job satisfaction. These correlations ranged from .61 for coworkers to .80 for supervision.

The JSS has also been shown to correlate with a number of scales and variables that have been shown in the literature to correlate with other job satisfaction scales. These include job characteristics as assessed with the JDS (Hackman & Oldham, 1975), age, organization level, absence, organizational commitment, leadership practices, intention to quit the job, and turnover (Spector, 1985).

Norms

Norms for the JSS are shown in Table 2.4. The table shows the mean subscale and total job satisfaction scores across many employees and many samples. The table indicates the number of samples, as well as the total number of respondents. Most samples represent a single organization, although several represent two or more organizations.

TABLE 2.4 Total Norms for the Job Satisfaction Survey

Subscale	Mean	Standard Deviation Across Samples
Pay	11.8	2.6
Promotion	12.0	1.9
Supervision	19.2	1.5
Benefits	14.2	2.2
Contingent rewards	13.7	2.0
Operating procedures	13.5	2.2
Coworkers	18.3	1.1
Nature of work	19.2	1.3
Communication	14.4	1.8
Total	136.5	12.1

NOTE: Norms based on 8,113 individuals from 52 samples.

The Job Descriptive Index (JDI)

The Job Descriptive Index (JDI; Smith, Kendall, & Hulin, 1969) has probably been the most popular facet scale among organizational researchers. It also may have been the most carefully developed and validated, as is well described in Smith et al.'s book. The scale assesses five facets:

1. Work
2. Pay
3. Promotion
4. Supervision
5. Coworkers

Many users of the scale have summed the five facet scores into an overall score, although this practice is not recommended by Smith and her associates (Ironson et al., 1989).

The entire scale contains 72 items with either 9 or 18 items per subscale. Each item is an evaluative adjective or short phrase that is descriptive of the job. Responses are "Yes," "Uncertain," or "No." For each facet scale, a brief explanation is provided, followed by the items concerning that facet. Both favorable or

(text continued on p. 14)

TABLE 2.5 Sample Items From the Job Descriptive Index (JDI)

Think of the work you do at present. How well does each of the following words or phrases describe your work? In the blank beside each word below, write

__Y__ for "Yes" if it describes your work

__N__ for "No" if it does NOT describe it

__?__ if you cannot decide

WORK ON PRESENT JOB

_____ Routine

_____ Satisfying

_____ Good

Think of the pay you get now. How well does each of the following words or phrases describe your present pay? In the blank beside each word below, write

__Y__ for "Yes" if it describes your pay

__N__ for "No" if it does NOT describe it

__?__ if you cannot decide

PRESENT PAY

_____ Income adequate for normal expenses

_____ Insecure

_____ Less than I deserve

Think of the opportunities for promotion that you have now. How well does each of the following words or phrases describe these? In the blank beside each word below, write

__Y__ for "Yes" if it describes your opportunities for promotion

__N__ for "No" if it does NOT describe them

__?__ if you cannot decide

OPPORTUNITIES FOR PROMOTION

_____ Dead-end job

_____ Unfair promotion policy

_____ Regular promotions

Think of the kind of supervision that you get on your job. How well does each of the following words or phrases describe this? In the blank beside each word below, write

__Y__ for "Yes" if it describes the supervision you get on your job

__N__ for "No" if it does NOT describe it

__?__ if you cannot decide

(continued)

TABLE 2.5 Continued

SUPERVISION

_____ Impolite

_____ Praises good work

_____ Doesn't supervise enough

Think of the majority of the people that you work with now or the people you meet in connection with your work. How well does each of the following words or phrases describe these people? In the blank beside each word below, write

__Y__ for "Yes" if it describes the people you work with

__N__ for "No" if it does NOT describe them

__?__ if you cannot decide

COWORKERS (PEOPLE)

_____ Boring

_____ Responsible

_____ Intelligent

SOURCE: From the Job Descriptive Index, which is copyrighted by Bowling Green State University. The complete forms, scoring key, instruction, and norms can be obtained from Dr. Patricia C. Smith, Department of Psychology, Bowling Green State University, Bowling Green, OH 43403.

positively worded and unfavorable or negatively worded items are provided. A sample of items from the JDI is in Table 2.5.

There is an extensive body of literature in which the scale has been used. Cook et al. (1981) listed more than 100 published studies that used the JDI. Thus, extensive normative data are available for potential users of the scale. The subscales also have very good reliabilities. The very extensive body of research using the scale provides good validation evidence. Perhaps the biggest limitation of the scale is that it is limited to five facets, although these are five of the most frequently assessed. In addition, there has been some criticism that particular items might not apply to all employee groups (e.g., Buffum & Konick, 1982; Cook et al., 1981). This criticism is probably true of all job satisfaction scales, however.

The reader should be aware that the JDI is copyrighted and a fee is required for its use. Permission to use the scale can be granted by Patricia C. Smith, Department of Psychology, Bowling Green State University, Bowling Green, OH 43403.

Although the JDI has very good psychometric properties, such as reliability and validity evidence, efforts have continued to improve it by both its developers and other researchers. Roznowski (1989) used sophisticated statistics to develop better items that would increase the reliability and validity of the scale. Smith and her colleagues have updated and improved the scale by replacing some of its items (Balzer et al., 1990). They also added a sixth scale of overall satisfaction called the JIG, which we will discuss later.

The Minnesota Satisfaction Questionnaire (MSQ)

The Minnesota Satisfaction Questionnaire (MSQ; Weiss et al., 1967) is another satisfaction scale that has been very popular among researchers. The MSQ comes in two forms, a 100-item long version and a 20-item short form. It covers 20 facets, many of which are more specific than most other satisfaction scales. The long form contains five items per facet, whereas the short form contains only one. Most researchers who use the short form combine all the items into a single total score, or compute extrinsic and intrinsic satisfaction subscales from subsets of items. Extrinsic satisfaction concerns aspects of work that have little to do with the job tasks or work itself, such as pay. Intrinsic satisfaction refers to the nature of job tasks themselves and how people feel about the work they do. Subscales, which have better reliabilities than individual items, are generally preferred.

The 20 facets of the MSQ are listed in Table 2.6. As can be seen, the facets are in many cases more specific than the JDI or JSS. For example, satisfaction with supervision is divided into an interpersonal or human relations component and a technical competence component. The nature of work itself is reflected in several facets, including ability utilization, achievement, activity, creativity, independence, and variety. Despite the greater specificity of the MSQ facets, much of its content is contained in other scales. For example, the JSS supervision items tap both the human relations and technical competence aspects. Note that the achievement item concerning a "feeling of accomplishment" is much like the last work facet item from the MSQ, which is "gives sense of accomplishment."

For the short form, several studies have reported acceptable internal consistency reliabilities for the extrinsic, intrinsic, and total scores. Some researchers have questioned the contents of the extrinsic and intrinsic subscales (Cook et al., 1981; Schriesheim, Powers, Scandura, Gardiner, & Landau, 1993). The lack of clear discriminability of the subscales is reflected in the rather high correlations between them found in several studies (e.g., $r = .83$ in Schmitt, Coyle, White, & Rauschenberger, 1978; $r = .63$ in Wexley, Alexander, Greenawalt, & Couch, 1980). Arvey and his associates (Arvey & Dewhirst, 1979; Arvey, Dewhirst, & Brown

TABLE 2.6 Facets From the Minnesota Satisfaction Questionnaire (MSQ)

Activity
Independence
Variety
Social status
Supervision (human relations)
Supervision (technical)
Moral values
Security
Social service
Authority
Ability utilization
Company policies and practices
Compensation
Advancement
Responsibility
Creativity
Working conditions
Coworkers
Recognition
Achievement

SOURCE: Weiss, Dawis, Lofquist, and England (1966).

1978; Zultowski, Arvey, & Dewhirst, 1978) have devised an alternative scoring scheme for the two subscales.

One question with the long form concerns the discriminability of some subscales. Many are highly intercorrelated suggesting that they may be assessing the same (or highly related) aspects of the job. For example, the two supervision scales were reported to correlate from .67 to .90 across samples by Weiss et al. (1967). Although we might wish to distinguish these two dimensions, employees might tend to feel the same about both aspects of their supervisors. On the positive side, corresponding subscales of the JDI and MSQ show good convergence (Gillet & Schwab, 1975).

Either form of the MSQ would certainly be a reasonable choice for the total scale, although the short form at one fifth the length would be sufficient. The two subscale scores from the short form should be used with caution, however, as

TABLE 2.7 Sample Items From the Job Diagnostic Survey Job Satisfaction Subscales

Facet	Item
Growth	The feeling of worthwhile accomplishment I get from doing my job
Pay	The amount of pay and fringe benefits I receive
Security	The amount of job security I have
Social	The people I talk to and work with on my job
Supervisor	The degree of respect and fair treatment I receive from my boss
General	Most people on this job are very satisfied with the job

SOURCE: Hackman and Oldham (1974).

discussed earlier. The long form would be a reasonable choice for assessing facets, provided that the facets included are those of interest. The scale is rather long at 100 items, contains facets that are more specific than most other scales, and covers the nature of work very thoroughly. One further note is that the scale is copyrighted. Copies can be purchased from the developers in the Psychology Department at the University of Minnesota. The long form costs $66 per hundred and the short form is $39 per hundred.

The Job Diagnostic Survey (JDS)

The Job Diagnostic Survey (JDS; Hackman & Oldham, 1975) is an instrument that was developed to study the effects of job characteristics on people. It contains subscales to measure the nature of the job and job tasks, motivation, personality, psychological states (cognitions and feelings about job tasks), and reactions to the job. One of the reactions is job satisfaction. The JDS is discussed here as a facet measure because it covers several areas of job satisfaction, specifically growth, pay, security, social, and supervision, as well as global satisfaction.

The individual subscales contain from two to five items each. The format for the facet items is a 7-point scale ranging from "Extremely dissatisfied" to "Extremely satisfied." The format for the global satisfaction subscale is a seven point ranging from "Disagree strongly" to "Agree strongly." Considering that its purpose was to study job characteristics, the JDS includes those facets that the authors felt were most important for this purpose. Sample items for each facet are in Table 2.7.

TABLE 2.8 Three Items From the Job In General Scale (JIG)

Think of your job in general. All in all, what is it like most of the time? In the blank beside each word or phrase below, write

__Y__ for "Yes" if it describes your job

__N__ for "No" if it does NOT describe it

__?__ if you cannot decide

JOB IN GENERAL

_____ Undesirable

_____ Better than most

_____ Rotten

SOURCE: From the Job in General Scale, which is copyrighted by Bowling Green State University. The complete forms, scoring key, instructions, and norms can be obtained from Dr. Patricia C. Smith, Department of Psychology, Bowling Green State University, Bowling Green, OH 43403.

The Job in General Scale (JIG)

The Job in General Scale (JIG; Ironson et al., 1989) was designed to assess overall job satisfaction rather than facets. Its format is the same as the JDI, and it contains 18 items. Each item is an adjective or short phrase about the job in general rather than a facet. The total score is a combination of all items. Ironson et al. argue that overall job satisfaction is not the sum of individual facets and that it should be assessed with a general scale like the JIG (see Table 2.8).

As with the JDI, the JIG uses three response choices. For each item, respondents are asked if they agree (yes), aren't sure (?) or disagree (no). Negatively worded items are reverse-scored, and the total score is the sum of the responses.

The JIG has good internal consistency reliability. Ironson et al. (1989) reported internal consistency coefficients from .91 to .95 across several samples. They also noted that the JIG correlates well with other global measures of job satisfaction.

The JIG would be a good choice for the assessment of overall job satisfaction when this is of interest rather than facets. Often, facet scales are used to assess general satisfaction by combining all of the individual facet scores. This can be justified by the fact that facets often correlate well with overall job satisfaction. For example, Ironson et al. (1989) found a .78 correlation of the JIG with the JDI work scale, and the JSS total score correlated .53 with the Michigan Organizational Assessment Questionnaire satisfaction scale, discussed in the next section (Spector, 1987). However, there have been critics of this practice (e.g., Ironson et al., 1989). The summing of subscale scores presumes that all facets have been assessed and

TABLE 2.9 Items From the Michigan Organizational Assessment Questionnaire Satisfaction Subscale

1. All in all I am satisfied with my job
2. In general, I don't like my job
3. In general, I like working here

that they each make an equal contribution to global satisfaction. It seems unlikely that each facet has the same importance to every individual. Thus, the sum of facets is an approximation of overall job satisfaction, but it may not exactly match the global satisfaction of individuals.

Michigan Organizational Assessment Questionnaire Subscale

The Michigan Organizational Assessment Questionnaire contains a three-item overall satisfaction subscale (Cammann et al., 1979). The scale is simple and short, which makes it ideal for use in questionnaires that contain many scales. The authors report an internal consistency reliability of .77, although subsequent studies have found higher reliabilities (e.g., .87; Jex & Gudanowski, 1992). The items of the scale are shown in Table 2.9.

For each item there are seven response choices: "Strongly disagree," "Disagree," "Slightly disagree," "Neither agree nor disagree," "Slightly agree," "Agree," "Strongly agree." The responses are numbered from 1 to 7, respectively, but the second item is reverse-scored. The items are totaled to yield an overall job satisfaction score. Validity evidence for the scale is provided by research in which it has been correlated with many other work variables (e.g., Jex & Gudanowski, 1992; Spector et al., 1988).

Developing or Modifying a Satisfaction Scale

Often, existing scales cannot be found to assess the job satisfaction facets one wishes to assess. Under those circumstances, one must develop new scales or modify an existing one. Although a detailed treatment of this topic is beyond the scope of this book, we will cover the basic steps involved in scale development.

Details can be found in other sources, such as DeVellis (1991) and Spector (1992b). One must be careful that appropriate permissions are acquired before modifying copyrighted scales. Although the procedure might seem relatively simple, it is best that one consult an expert in scale development the first time a scale development project is undertaken to oversee the procedures that are used.

All of the scales discussed in this book used multiple items as opposed to single items. Although the short form of the MSQ has a single item per facet, the items were combined into multiple-item subscales. If one is interested in several facets, this can result in rather long scales. It is reasonable to ask why one cannot use a single question per facet.

There are two good reasons to use multiple items. First, and most important, multiple-item scales are more reliable than single items. This is because respondents can make mistakes when filling out questionnaires. Errors can be produced when a respondent interprets a question differently than intended. For example, the item "I like my boss" might be intended to refer to the immediate supervisor, but some individuals might assume it refers to the top-level manager of the organization. In other cases, a person might misread an item. A common error is for a person to miss a "not" in an item. For example, the item "I do not like my pay" might be seen as "I do like my pay." Individuals also can interpret the item correctly but make a mistake and indicate the wrong response. For example, a person might mean to indicate "Agree strongly" and mistakenly circle the 1 instead of the 6. Mistakes that occur more or less randomly across people can produce inconsistencies in scores for the same people over time. A person who mistakenly scores high on one occasion might correctly score low on another.

The larger the number of items in a subscale, the smaller the effect of inconsistent responses to items over time. With a single item, an error can move a person's score from one end of the scale to the other. With multiple items, an error can move a person's score only a portion of the total range of scores. With 10 items, each item contributes only 10% of the total score. What this produces is more stability in scores over time, and hence, more reliability.

Second, multiple items allow for a more complete assessment of a facet. What may seem to be a simple facet can have a number of aspects to it. A single item may not do a good job of covering all aspects. For example, a person may be able to indicate their overall satisfaction with pay in a single item, but pay includes many aspects that would take several items to cover. There is the amount of pay, amount of raises, frequency of raises, fairness of pay, pay policies, sufficiency to meet financial needs, future prospects for increases, and relations to performance. An individual who answers a single item might do so in response to only some of

TABLE 2.10 Five Steps for Developing a Satisfaction Scale

Step 1	Carefully and thoroughly define the facet
Step 2	Design scale format and write items
Step 3	Pilot test items on small sample
Step 4	Administer items to large sample and item analyze
Step 5	Compile norms and validation evidence on multiple samples

these aspects. Multiple items allow for more specific questions and allow for the more complete assessment of the facet.

Procedure for Scale Development

The complete development of a satisfaction scale is a five-step process. Table 2.10 lists the steps involved in such an undertaking. The first step is to define carefully and completely the facet or facets of interest. It is here that many scale development efforts are compromised because the exact nature of the construct of interest was left ambiguous and incompletely described. There are two major ways in which a facet can be delineated and developed. First, the scale developers can consult their own experience to define the various aspects of a facet. Second, interviews with employed people can be conducted to help define the various aspects. When a scale is developed for use in a particular organization, it is not uncommon to interview a sample of employees from that organization to help define the facets of interest.

Once the facet is clearly defined, items can be written to assess each aspect. If the facet has multiple aspects to it, one or more items can be written to assess each facet. The better and more thorough the job done on defining the aspect, the easier it will be to write items. A good item is a clear, concise, concrete statement that reflects either something favorable or unfavorable about a job or an aspect of the job. Part of the item generation step is to choose a format for the scale. For example, will the scale have the checklist look of the JDI or the summated rating scale format of the MSQ?

The third step is to administer the new items to a small sample to pilot test them. The purpose of this is to be sure that the items are clear and understandable. The fourth step is to administer the scale and conduct an item analysis. An item analysis is a statistical procedure that is used to determine the items that work best in the scale from the perspective of internal consistency reliability. This means that items are chosen that tend to intercorrelate with one another. A statistic called the item-total correlation is computed for each item to show how well it relates to all other items.

The final step is to validate the scale and compile norms. This last step is one that is often skipped when scales are developed for applied uses in organizations. This is because it can be quite difficult and time consuming to conduct validation studies. It is a requirement for publication of research papers about the development of new job satisfaction scales. Validation is always a good idea, however, to demonstrate that the interpretation of results is correct. Admittedly, constraints in organizations often do not allow for this to be done.

3

How People
Feel About Work

Every few years the Gallup Organization conducts a survey to determine how Americans feel about their jobs and issues related to employment. Similar surveys are conducted in Canada and other countries.

Surveys conducted in the United States generally show that most Americans are satisfied with their jobs overall. In a 1991 Gallup Poll, 83% of respondents reported that they were satisfied with their jobs (Hugick & Leonard, 1991). Feelings about the job, as well as other aspects of life, are likely to vary across different countries, however. A recent Gallup Organization (1995) poll found country differences in life satisfaction, which included job satisfaction. Overall, 46% of people in 18 countries throughout the world reported being satisfied with their jobs.

The 1991 survey of Americans included 16 aspects of work, as well as overall satisfaction. For each work aspect, respondents were asked to indicate its importance and how satisfied they were with it. The results showed that the majority of

TABLE 3.1 Sixteen Features of Jobs Listed From Most to Least Importance for
Americans and the Percentage of People Satisfied With Each One

Having good health insurance and other benefits	67
Having interesting work	88
Having job security	79
Having the opportunity to learn new skills	88
Being able to take vacations of a week or more during the year	88
Being able to work independently	89
Having your accomplishments recognized by the people you work with	76
Having a job in which you can help others	83
Limiting the amount of on-the-job stress	62
Having regular hours—that is, not being scheduled to work nights and weekends	86
Earning a high income	66
Working close to home	87
Doing work that is important to society	83
Chances for promotion	60
Having a lot of contact with people	91
Having flexible hours	83

SOURCE: Hugick and Leonard (1991).

Americans liked their jobs overall (Hugick & Leonard, 1991). However, they did
not feel the same about all facets of work. Table 3.1 lists the 16 facets and the
percentage of people who indicated being satisfied with them. The facets are listed
in order from most to least important, according to the respondents. The largest
percentage of people were satisfied with aspects that involved the nature of the
work itself. Most people were satisfied with how interesting the work is and the
amount of contact with other people. Far fewer were satisfied with rewards, such
as fringe benefits and promotion opportunities.

The typical American pattern of facet satisfaction also can be seen in the Job
Satisfaction Survey norms in Table 2.4. The typical American pattern is to be
satisfied with coworkers, the nature of work itself, and supervision but not very
satisfied with rewards, such as fringe benefits and pay. Some of the reason for this
might be that Americans tend to expect to advance at work and experience an
increase in standard of living as a reward for hard work. Thus, they are often
somewhat dissatisfied with their career and salary progress. These findings are
consistent with the Gallup results. They are not consistent with results found in all
countries, as we will discuss in the next section on cultural differences in job
satisfaction.

Cultural and Demographic Differences in Job Satisfaction

Age

Research has shown that age and job satisfaction are related. The exact nature of the relation is not clear, as some studies have found a curvilinear, wheras others have found a linear relation. Brush, Moch, and Pooyan (1987) conducted a meta-analysis of 19 studies that had a mean correlation of .22 between age and job satisfaction. These studies show that in general job satisfaction increases with age. Zeitz (1990) found a curvilinear relation in which job satisfaction declines early in life, levels off in middle age, and rebounds after approximately 45 years of age. Not all studies, however, have been able to find evidence for a curvilinear relation (e.g., White & Spector, 1987).

A factor that might be important in the age-job satisfaction relation is gender. Clark, Oswald, and Warr (1996) surveyed more than 5000 men and women in an English study. They found clear curvilinear relations of age with global job satisfaction, as well as nature of work and pay facets for men. For women, the curvilinear pattern was of small magnitude for global job satisfaction and did not exist for either facet. Only a linear relation was found. Furthermore, the curvilinear pattern for men would not have been apparent had the age distribution not begun at late teens for this sample.

The Clark et al. (1996) study suggests that age distribution and gender composition of samples can affect whether or not the curvilinear pattern is detected. An adequate sample for this purpose should range in age from late teens to late 60s and contain few women. An additional factor that affects these tests is that statistical techniques to detect curvilinear relations generally have lower power than do procedures to detect linear patterns. Failure to find significant curvilinear trends might be caused in some cases by relatively low statistical power due to insufficient sample size rather than linearity (Bedeian, Ferris, & Kacmar, 1992).

Whether the relation is curvilinear or linear, it is important to understand the reasons that age relates to job satisfaction. Little is known about the causes for this observed relation, but several hypotheses have been advanced. Wright and Hamilton (1978) proposed two likely mechanisms. First, the cohort mechanism is that expectations and values of Americans have changed over time. Older workers are more satisfied with their jobs than younger workers because they are more accepting of authority and expect less from their jobs. Second, the job change mechanism is that older workers have better jobs and more skill than their younger counterparts. Two other possibilities are that over time people have more "sunk costs" or investment in a job, and expectations can change over time. The first mechanism suggests that with time, the investment in the job in terms of benefits (e.g., pension) and rewards (e.g., pay) might contribute to job satisfaction. The latter is that people adapt to the job by adjusting their expectations to be more realistic, so that they are happier with less as they get older.

An adequate test of the cohort mechanism apparently does not yet exist. It would require a long-term longitudinal study in which a sample of people would be assessed throughout life to determine if their job satisfaction was related to age. The job change mechanism has received at least some empirical support. White and Spector (1987) showed that the age-job satisfaction relation could be explained by better job conditions for older workers. The older worker reported a closer match between what he or she had and wanted in terms of job conditions as well as higher salary. They also perceived a higher level of personal control over job rewards. Little research evidence exists that addresses the remaining two hypothesized mechanisms.

Country Differences

Comparisons have been made of the job satisfaction of employees from different countries, although the number of countries compared has been very limited. For example, Slocum and Topichak (1972) reported that Mexicans were more satisfied with their jobs than Americans, and Marion-Landais (1993) found that Dominicans were more satisfied than Americans who worked for branches of the same company in their own countries. However, Griffeth and Hom (1987) found that Latin American managers were less satisfied than managers from western Europe. Several studies have shown that Japanese workers are less satisfied than Americans (e.g., Lincoln, Hanada, & Olson, 1981; see also review by Smith & Misumi, 1989). Spector and Wimalasiri (1986) found that Americans and Singaporeans did not differ in their global job satisfaction.

There have been only a handful of country comparisons of job satisfaction facets using the same scale. Table 3.2 shows results for the JSS subscales for the Dominican Republic, Hong Kong, Singapore, and the United States. The Dominican Republic scored highest on all facets except operating procedures, for which it was second lowest. Hong Kong, Singapore, and the United States had approximately the same global job satisfaction, but the facet profiles were different. Hong Kong had the flattest profile, with mean job satisfaction scores ranging from 12.1 to 16 on a scale that ranged from 4 to 24. Singapore scored highest of all four

TABLE 3.2 Job Satisfaction Facet Comparisons Across Four Countries on the JSS

Facet	Dominican Republic	Hong Kong	Singapore	United States
Pay	17.2	15.0	14.0	11.9
Promotion	16.4	14.2	13.4	11.8
Supervision	20.0	16.0	13.4	19.0
Benefits	16.8	14.4	14.2	14.4
Contingent rewards	17.8	14.9	17.3	13.6
Procedures	12.3	12.1	17.0	13.5
Coworkers	20.0	15.6	13.4	18.1
Work	22.2	14.9	17.1	19.1
Communication	18.1	14.9	14.9	14.2
Total	160.9	133.3	134.7	135.8
Sample size	148	136	182	12,748

SOURCES: The Dominican data were from Marion-Landais (1993); the Hong Kong data were from Lammond (1995); the Singapore data were from Spector and Wimalasiri (1986); and the U.S. data were the unpublished norms for the JSS available from the author.

countries in operating procedures, and its highest facet was contingent rewards. Both Asian countries scored higher than the United States in the reward areas of pay and promotion but lower in nature of work and the two social facets of coworkers and supervision.

The U.S. profile had the greatest variability. The United States scored lowest of the four countries in the reward areas of contingent rewards (e.g., appreciation and recognition for good work), pay, and promotion opportunities. Americans scored quite high in coworkers, nature of work, and supervision. These results show that even where countries might not show differences in overall job satisfaction, there can be large differences among facets.

These studies show clearly that there are differences in job satisfaction and in patterns of facet satisfaction across countries. They do not provide much insight into the reasons for differences, which could be caused by different cultural experiences and practices in the workplace. For example, work conditions might be better in some countries than others. They might also be attributable to different expectations of people. For example, Americans tend to believe that they should advance at work. When they do not, they are likely to be dissatisfied with promotion opportunities. In other countries, people might accept the fact that they are not likely to be promoted, so they are not unhappy when promotions are not available. Biases can also be a factor in these studies. Marion-Landais (1993) argued that one reason for the high job satisfaction in his Dominican sample may have been that his subjects were fearful about expressing dissatisfaction. They may have inflated their job satisfaction ratings, to avoid seeming critical of their employers. Finally, many of these studies did not have identical samples for inter-country comparisons. Thus, organizational level (manager vs. nonmanager) and type of work were not always controlled. However, it seems likely that job satisfaction differences across different countries are real. Additional research is badly needed to help us understand how people in different countries feel about work.

Gender

Relations between gender and job satisfaction have been extremely inconsistent across studies. When results of different studies are combined with meta-analysis, mean correlations tend to be almost zero across dozens of studies and thousands of people (Brush et al., 1987; Witt & Nye, 1992). In other words, men and women have the same levels of job satisfaction. What is surprising about these results is that men and women in these studies do not have the same jobs. For example, Greenhaus, Parasuraman, and Wormley (1990) found no significant gender differences in job satisfaction, even though the females in their study were less likely to have managerial/professional jobs and more likely to have low-paid clerical jobs than the males.

Several explanations have been advanced to explain the equivalent job satisfaction of women to men despite nonequivalent job conditions and pay. First, it has been suggested that women may differ in expectations (Brush et al., 1987). Women expect less from work and so they are satisfied with less. This may have developed over generations in which women had to accept fewer promotion opportunities and lower pay even for the same jobs. Second, men and women might have different values. Witt and Nye (1992) discussed how there can be gender differences in perceptions of equity. Men and women sometimes view fairness in reward distribution differently. Again, this could lead to women perceiving lesser rewards as being more fair than would men. Although these are possible explanations, at present it is not clear why women have equivalent job satisfaction despite nonequivalent work.

Racial Differences in the United States

As with gender, there has been inconsistency in results comparing black and white Americans' job satisfaction. In a few studies, the job satisfaction of blacks was lower than whites (e.g., Greenhaus et al., 1990; Tuch & Martin, 1991). However, in Brush et al.'s (1987) meta-analysis, no evidence was found for racial differences across 15 studies. It should be noted that this meta-analysis restricted itself to unpublished data available to the authors.

The two studies noted earlier that found racial differences also found differences in other variables. In the Greenhaus et al. (1990) study, the black employees reported receiving lower performance appraisal ratings than their white counterparts. The reason for this difference was not discussed, but it alone might have caused the job satisfaction differences observed. Tuch and Martin (1991) used samples from national surveys of the U.S. population. Although black respondents were slightly lower in job satisfaction, there were also racial differences on other important variables. Blacks in the sample were more likely to be in blue collar jobs, live in cities, live in the South, and perceive fewer rewards at work. The authors argued that blacks and whites do not differ in the underlying mechanisms that lead to job satisfaction. The failure to find racial differences in some studies may have been due to the greater similarity of jobs across races in these samples than in studies where differences have been found.

Antecedents of Job Satisfaction

Antecedents of job satisfaction can be classified into two major categories. First, the job environment itself and factors associated with the job are important influences on job satisfaction. This includes how people are treated, the nature of job tasks, relations with other people in the workplace, and rewards. Second, there are individual factors that the person brings to the job. This includes both personality and prior experiences. Both categories of antecedents often work together to influence employee job satisfaction. The fit between the individual and the job has been shown to be an important influence on employee job satisfaction (Kristof, 1996).

Environmental Antecedents of Job Satisfaction

Job Characteristics and Job Characteristics Theory

It has long been believed that routine, simple jobs such as we find on the traditional assembly line are inherently boring and dissatisfying (see Hulin & Blood, 1968). Many have advocated job redesign as a means of enhancing job satisfaction by making jobs more interesting (e.g., Herzberg, 1968; Herzberg, Mausner, & Snyderman, 1959). This is done by changing the characteristics of a person's job and tasks. Job characteristics refer to the content and nature of job tasks themselves. There are only a few different characteristics studied as contributors to job satisfaction (Wall & Martin, 1987).

The most influential theory of how job characteristics affect people is Hackman and Oldham's job characteristics theory (Hackman & Oldham, 1976, 1980). The basis of job characteristics theory is that people can be motivated by the intrinsic satisfaction they find in doing job tasks. When they find their work to be enjoyable and meaningful, people will like their jobs and will be motivated to perform their jobs well. The theory is illustrated in Figure 4.1. It shows how core characteristics of jobs induce psychological states that in turn lead to job performance, job satisfaction, motivation, and turnover. The five core characteristics can be applied to any job:

1. Skill variety
2. Task identity
3. Task significance
4. Autonomy
5. Job feedback

They are defined in Table 4.1.

The five core characteristics are thought to lead to three psychological states. Skill variety, task identity, and task significance combined induce experienced meaningfulness of work. Autonomy leads to feelings of responsibility. Feedback results in knowledge of results about the products of work. The three psychological states in turn contribute to important outcomes of job satisfaction and motivation of employees.

According to job characteristics theory, the five core characteristics determine how motivating a job is likely to be. The Motivation Potential Score or MPS for a

(text continued on p. 33)

32

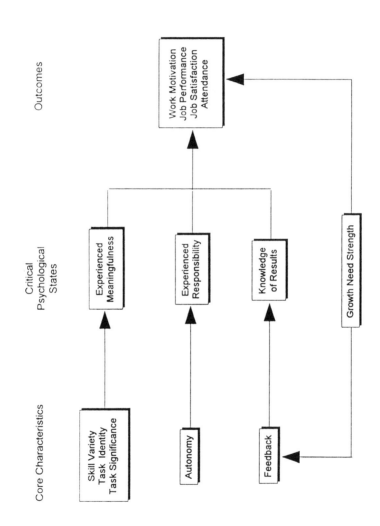

Figure 4.1. Hackman and Oldham's (1976) Job Characteristics Model

TABLE 4.1 Dimensions of Job Characteristics

Mean Characteristic	Description of Characteristic
Skill variety	The number of different skills necessary to do a job
Task identity	Whether or not an employee does an entire job or a piece of a job
Task significance	The impact a job has on other people
Autonomy	The freedom employees have to do their jobs as they see fit
Job feedback	The extent to which it is obvious to employees that they are doing their jobs correctly
Job scope	The overall complexity of a job, computed as a combination of all five individual characteristics

job reflects complexity or scope. The MPS is determined by mathematically combining scores on the five core characteristics, using the following formula:

$$MPS = (S.V. + T.I. + T.S.)/3 \times Auton. \times Feed.$$

where S.V. = skill variety, T.I. = task identity, T.S. = task significance, Auton. = autonomy, and Feed. = feedback. The first three core characteristics are averaged, and that average is multiplied by the other two. The higher the MPS score or scope of a job, the more motivating and satisfying it will be. The multiplicative nature of this formula implies that a job must induce all three psychological states to be motivating. If one of the three multiplicative terms in the equation is equal to zero, the job will not be at all motivating.

Hackman and Oldham (1976) included a personality variable in their theory. Growth need strength or GNS was hypothesized to be a moderator of the effects of the core characteristics. A moderator is a variable that influences the relation between other variables. Earlier we discussed research showing that the relation between age and job satisfaction was different for men and women. In this case, gender would be said to moderate the relation between age and job satisfaction.

The GNS variable reflects an individual's need for fulfillment of higher order needs, such as autonomy or personal growth. The theory states that the motivating effects of job characteristics will occur only for individuals who are high in GNS. Although they did not discuss people who were low, it is assumed that they did not expect such individuals to be motivated by jobs that were high on MPS. Figure 4.2 illustrates how the relation between MPS and job satisfaction is moderated by GNS.

Simply put, the job characteristics theory states that people who prefer challenge and interest in their work will be happier and more motivated if they have complex jobs, as defined by the five core characteristics. Such people would be likely to avoid very simple jobs, however, and might be attracted to managerial or professional work that provides higher levels of complexity.

Hackman and Oldham (1975) developed the Job Diagnostic Survey or JDS to assess all of the variables in their theory. This scale has been the most popular measure of job characteristics among researchers in this field. The JDS also included the measure of job satisfaction that we discussed in Chapter 2. Other measures of job characteristics also have been developed. The most popular alternative measure is the Job Characteristics Index or JCI (Sims, Szilagyi, & Keller, 1976), which assesses four of the five JDS characteristics (Autonomy, Feedback, Skill variety, and Task identity). The JCI tends to have better reliability than the JDS, primarily due to its greater number of items per subscale (Fried, 1991).

Campion and his colleagues (Campion, 1988, 1989; Campion & Thayer, 1985) have developed a more extensive instrument to assess characteristics of jobs. Their Multimethod Job Design Questionnaire goes far beyond the five dimensions of the JDS to provide a more complete picture of a job. Campion's scale assesses not only the motivational potential of a job but its physical features as well. It covers the four areas of motivational, mechanistic, biological, and perceptual-motor features. A job could be very high in motivation potential because it contains high levels of the core characteristics but be very poorly designed in terms of mental or physical requirements reflected by the other three areas. For example, a job that requires heavy lifting might be too difficult for most people to do, or a job that requires the use of poorly designed tools could lead to serious physical injury.

Most job characteristics studies have used measures such as the JDS completed by job incumbents to assess the job. These studies have found that incumbent reports of job characteristics significantly correlate with job satisfaction and motivation. Meta-analyses that mathematically combine results across studies provide estimates of how strongly these measures are related. Fried and Ferris (1987) analyzed results of almost 200 studies. Table 4.2 summarizes the findings relating the five characteristics to both global and growth satisfaction. As can be seen, correlations tended to be larger for growth than global satisfaction. For global satisfaction, they ranged from .20 for task identity to .34 for autonomy. The table also shows correlations of growth satisfaction with the four job characteristics from the JCI. Campion and McClelland (1991) found evidence that physical characteristics of jobs are also important contributors to job satisfaction.

Meta-analyses have also supported the hypothesized role of growth need strength (Loher, Noe, Moeller, & Fitzgerald, 1985). Studies have found larger

(text continued on p. 36)

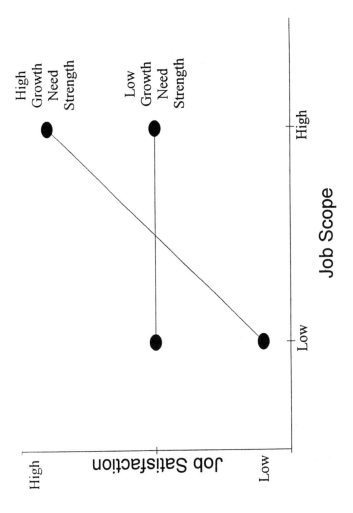

Figure 4.2. Graph Showing the Moderating Effect of Growth Need Strength on the Job Scope-Job Satisfaction Relation

NOTE: Scope is represented by the horizontal axis of the graph. Job satisfaction is on the vertical axis. For people high in growth need strength, satisfaction is high when scope is high and low when scope is low. For people who are low in growth need strength, satisfaction is unaffected by level of job scope.

TABLE 4.2 Mean Correlations of Job Characteristics With Global Job Satisfaction and Growth Satisfaction for the JCI and JDS

Job Characteristic	Global Satisfaction With JDS	Growth Satisfaction With JDS	Growth Satisfaction With JCI
Autonomy	.34	.50	.28
Feedback	.29	.40	.36
Skill variety	.29	.45	.54
Task identity	.20	.25	.29
Task significance	.26	.35	na

SOURCES: JCI correlations were from Fried (1991). JDS correlations were from Fried and Ferris (1987).

correlations between job characteristics and job satisfaction for people who are high than people who are low on this personality variable.

There have been many critics of JDS based research to test the hypotheses of job characteristics theory (e.g., Frese & Zapf, 1988; Roberts & Glick, 1981; Spector, 1992a; Taber & Taylor, 1990). Much of the criticism has concerned what the incumbent measures such as the JDS actually measure. Both Spector (1992a) and Taber and Taylor (1990) discussed evidence that incumbent measures may be affected by many things other than job characteristics. For example, people who like their jobs are likely to perceive them as higher in scope than their counterparts who dislike their jobs, just because they like them. Another problem is that most studies in this area merely demonstrate that job characteristics are correlated with job satisfaction. It has not been established that this relation is in any way causal. In other words, it is not clear that job characteristics actually lead to job satisfaction. It is possible, as noted earlier, that many findings are due to the opposite possibility that job satisfaction affects people's perceptions of job characteristics. Although many of the findings we have discussed are suggestive that job characteristics contribute to job satisfaction, other types of studies are needed to test this hypothesis.

Although research with incumbent reports has been fairly consistent, results using other methods have been less so. Experiments have been conducted in both laboratory and field settings to see if manipulations of job characteristics would affect job satisfaction and other hypothesized outcomes. Some of these studies have found that these outcomes were affected as hypothesized by job scope (e.g., Ganster, 1980; Griffin, 1991; Kim, 1980; Orpen, 1979; Wall, Corbett, Martin, Clegg, & Jackson, 1990). Others have found nonsignificant or weak effects (e.g., Griffeth, 1985; Lawler, Hackman, & Kaufman, 1973).

Several researchers have used nonincumbent measures of job characteristics, such as observer or supervisor ratings of jobs. Results of these studies have found inconsistent correlations of job characteristics with job satisfaction. For example, Spector and Jex (1991) compared incumbent JDS ratings with job characteristics data generated by job analysts who never met the incumbents. Although the incumbent measures of job characteristics correlated significantly with job satisfaction, the analyst measures did not. Glick, Jenkins, and Gupta (1986) found that observers' ratings of job characteristics correlated modestly with job satisfaction (multiple $R = .15$). Incumbent ratings correlated much higher with job satisfaction (multiple $R = .43$).

One reason for inconsistencies of results may have been the focus on JDS dimensions in most studies. Melamed, Ben-Avi, Luz, and Green (1995) operationalized job characteristics as task cycle time for a factory worker, which is the amount of time it takes to do the job. Cycle time is relevant to monotony, as repetitive jobs have tasks with the shortest cycle times. They found that the longer the cycle time for a job, the greater the job satisfaction.

Griffin (1991) conducted a longitudinal study of a job redesign in an organization. His results showed that job satisfaction increased immediately following the job change. However, it returned to the prechange level by the end of a 2-year follow-up. Interestingly, scores on the JDS increased after the change and were maintained at the 2-year assessment. These results suggest that the job change was perceived by employees even after 2 years, but the impact of the job characteristics was transitory. This result is consistent with an expectancy or Hawthorne effect. Job satisfaction may have improved just because management was paying attention to the well-being of employees. The nature of the change may have had little to do with the outcome. In fact, evidence exists that anticipation of change can have more of an effect on job satisfaction than the change itself (Salancik & Pfeffer, 1978). For example, a management announcement of an upcoming improvement at work can itself be seen as something very positive by employees, who then would report enhanced job satisfaction for at least a short time.

It seems likely from the existing research that job characteristics affect job satisfaction. However, it also seems likely that not everyone responds favorably to jobs that are high in job scope or MPS. The design of jobs that maximizes employee job satisfaction is difficult and must consider the personalities of employees. Employee job satisfaction is likely to be positively related to job characteristics when employees have input into those characteristics either through input into their job's design or by job choice. In other words, job satisfaction is likely to be high when people have the job characteristics that they prefer.

TABLE 4.3   The Eight Peters and O'Connor (1980) Organizational
                      Constraint Areas

Job-related information. Information needed for the job.

Tools and equipment. Tools and equipment necessary for the job.

Materials and supplies. Materials and supplies necessary for the job.

Budgetary support. Money necessary to acquire resources to do the job.

Required services and help from others. Help available from other people.

Task preparation. Whether or not the employee has the skills necessary for the job.

Time availability. The amount of time available for doing the job.

Work environment. The physical features of the job environment.

Organizational Constraints

Conditions of the job environment that interfere with employee job performance are called organizational constraints. The constraints come from many aspects
of the job, including other people and the physical work environment. Peters,
O'Connor, and Rudolf (1980) used the critical incident technique to develop a
taxonomy of constraint areas. They surveyed 62 working people about their
experience with organizational constraints on the job. Each participant described
a constraint incident that interfered with their job performance. A content analysis
of the responses was used to derive the eight areas shown in Table 4.3.

Although the major focus of organizational constraints research has been on
job performance (Peters & O'Connor, 1980), it has been shown to relate to job
satisfaction, as well. Employees who perceive high levels of constraints tend to be
dissatisfied with their jobs. Significant relations have been found between various
measures of constraints and job satisfaction (e.g., Jex & Gudanowski, 1992;
Keenan & Newton, 1984; O'Connor et al., 1984; Spector et al., 1988). O'Connor,
Peters, Rudolf, and Pooyan (1982) reported correlations of organizational constraints with five job satisfaction facets (coworker = −.30, pay = −.26, promotion
= −.28, supervision = −.42, and work itself = −.31). The largest correlation with
supervision satisfaction likely reflects that supervisors are the biggest source of
constraints as seen by subordinates. Although these results might be interpreted as
reflecting the effects of the job environment on employees, the reliance on
incumbent self-report methods makes this conclusion tentative until additional
methodologies are used.

Role Variables

One approach to viewing the interaction of employees and jobs is from the perspective of roles (Katz & Kahn, 1978). A role is the required pattern of behavior for an individual in the organization. Organizational roles can be associated with job positions or titles, but they are not identical, as each individual can have several roles, and not everyone with the same job title has the same role in all cases. For example, one person in an office might have the role of managing the coffee pot and supplies, even though it is not a formal part of the job. Often, the person develops the role by taking on a task that others then assume will become that person's responsibility.

Role theory researchers have developed variables hypothesized to be important influences on job satisfaction. Role ambiguity and role conflict have been the most thoroughly studied.

Role ambiguity is the degree of certainty the employee has about what his or her functions and responsibilities are. In many jobs, the expectations of supervisors concerning the subordinate's roles are not clearly delineated, leading to employee role ambiguity.

Role conflict exists when people experience incompatible demands about their functions and responsibilities. Intra-role conflict occurs when the conflict involves different people at work or different functions. This happens when two supervisors make demands that conflict or when the individual must accomplish two things but has time to accomplish only one of them. For example, one supervisor might ask an employee to run an errand while at the same time another asks the employee to take a phone call.

Extra-role conflict occurs when there are conflicts between work and non-work. The most frequently discussed form of extra-role conflict occurs between family and work responsibilities. A child might be sick on the day that the parent has a big presentation to make. This form of role conflict can be especially troublesome for couples with children who are both employed out of the home.

Both role ambiguity and role conflict have been shown to correlate with job satisfaction. Most studies of role variables have been surveys with role ambiguity and role conflict assessed with questionnaires. In their meta-analysis, Jackson and Schuler (1985) found mean correlations with global job satisfaction of $-.30$ and $-.31$ for role ambiguity and role conflict, respectively. With job satisfaction facets, supervision satisfaction had the largest correlation, $r = -.36$ for both role variables. This probably reflects that supervisors are the greatest source of role ambiguity and role conflict at work. The weakest correlation was with pay satisfaction, which had a −.17 correlation with role ambiguity and a −.20 correlation with role conflict.

As with job characteristics, the survey results are only weak evidence that role variables have an impact on job satisfaction. There have been very few studies that have used more conclusive methodologies. One attempt was a laboratory study by Hall (1990), who experimentally manipulated role ambiguity for college students who completed an in-basket exercise. This exercise is a paper-and-pencil problem-solving task that is commonly found in assessment centers to select managers. She found no effect of role ambiguity on job satisfaction in her study. Of course, student reactions in the laboratory might be different from those of employees at work. Additional research in this area is badly needed.

Work-Family Conflict

Work-family conflict exists when demands of the family and demands of the job interfere with one another. The problem can occur for anyone with a family but is especially troublesome for two-career couples with children and for single parents. Conflict is likely when children are sick and when school activities require parent involvement. It is likely that work-family conflict affects men and women differently because women usually assume more of the child-rearing role than men.

According to the 1991 Gallup poll, 34% of Americans experience a considerable amount of work-family conflict (Hugick & Leonard, 1991). A question was included about what people believed to be the best family versus work situation. Only 14% of both men and women felt that both parents should work outside of the home. An additional 39% said that one parent should work while the other stayed home to take care of children. Apparently, Americans are quite sensitive to the problems of work-family conflict.

Work-family conflict has been found to correlate significantly with job satisfaction. Employees who experience high levels of conflict tend to report low levels of job satisfaction (e.g., Bedeian, Burke, & Moffett, 1988; Holahan & Gilbert, 1979; Lewis & Cooper, 1987; Rice, Frone, & McFarlin, 1992). It is possible that there are gender differences in the relation between conflict and job satisfaction. Parasuraman, Greenhaus, and Granrose (1992) found that for men but not women work-family conflict correlated significantly with job satisfaction. For men, conflict correlated with job satisfaction −.40, whereas the corresponding correlation for their employed wives was −.02.

Several possible reasons for this difference between men and women exist. First, women might be better able to juggle demands of family and job so that work-family conflict has less impact on their work attitudes. Second, men might be more sensitive to work-family conflict than women are, and therefore, they experience more negative attitudinal reactions. Third, perhaps women place less importance on work so conflicts bother them less than they do men. The 1991 Gallup work survey found that men attributed more importance to work than did women (Hugick & Leonard, 1991). This may result in men having more conflicts between the family and the workplace. Fourth, men and women may have had different job experiences.

Beatty (1996) studied work-family conflict in a sample of Canadian professional women. Contrary to the results of Parasuraman et al. (1992), there was a significant correlation between work-family conflict and job satisfaction of –.20 for these women. The findings here that women demonstrated a correlation between conflict and job satisfaction provide support for the job importance explanation of gender differences in correlations. Professional women undoubtedly consider their jobs to be very important, resulting in decreased job satisfaction when work-family conflict occurs.

Stewart and Barling (1996) conducted a study to explore the impact of work-family conflict and job satisfaction on parenting behavior in a sample of employed fathers. Work-family conflict correlated –.39 with job satisfaction, which in turn correlated significantly with parental practices. They used complex statistical procedures (structural equation modeling) to test a model they developed showing how conflict affects the children of employed parents. They found evidence that conflict contributes to job satisfaction, which leads to parental practice, which affects children's performance in school. This study demonstrates that there can be important ramifications of work conditions and job satisfaction that extend beyond the workplace.

Organizations can adopt policies that either help people cope with or reduce work-family conflict. Thomas and Ganster (1995) studied the impact of organizational policies and supervisor behavior on employee experience of work-family conflict and job satisfaction. Their research provides evidence that organizational policies such as child care and flexible work schedules can reduce work-family conflict and enhance job satisfaction. Behavior by supervisors that supports employees with family responsibilities was also found to have positive effects. Organizations can often help employees reduce work-family conflict by adopting "family friendly" policies that are inexpensive, such as offering flexibility in work scheduling. Even without formal policies, supervisors in many organizations have discretion to allow flexibility that reduces at least some work-family conflict.

Pay

The correlation between level of pay and job satisfaction tends to be surprisingly small. As might be expected, level of pay correlates more strongly with pay satisfaction than global job satisfaction. Spector (1985) found a mean correlation of only .17 between level of pay and job satisfaction in three samples representing a heterogeneous collection of jobs. This small correlation suggests that pay itself is not a very strong factor in job satisfaction.

Although pay level is not an important issue, pay fairness can be very important. Most employees are not concerned that people in other jobs make more than they do. They are often quite concerned that people in the same job earn more. Rice, Phillips, and McFarlin (1990) reported a moderately large correlation of .50 between pay level and job satisfaction in a sample of mental health professionals who all had the same job. In a homogeneous sample, people are likely to compare themselves to one another and be quite dissatisfied if their salary is lower than others in the same job. What can be even more important than salary differences, however, is procedural justice in pay policies. This means that people should perceive the policies and procedures by which salary is administered to be fair, even if it results in differential pay. In other words, the process can have a bigger impact on job satisfaction than the actual levels of pay.

Job Stress

On every job there will be conditions and situations that employees find to be stressful. Being yelled at by an irate customer or having a machine break while rushing to meet a deadline are stressful events that can be common for certain jobs. Warr and Payne (1983) conducted a survey of working adults in Britain in which they asked if they had been emotionally upset by something that happened the prior day at work. Of those surveyed, 15% of men and 10% of women indicated having been upset by work. These sorts of situations can affect not only transitory emotional states but more long-term job satisfaction as well. Evidence has also been found that job stress can have a detrimental impact on both physical health and emotional well-being (Cooper & Cartwright, 1994).

There are two important categories of variables in job stress research. A job stressor is a condition or event at work that requires an adaptive response by a person, such as being yelled at or having to complete a difficult assignment by a particular deadline. A job strain is the response to a job stressor, such as the emotion of anxiety or the physical symptom of a headache. Jex and Beehr (1991) categorized strains into behavioral reactions (e.g., quitting the job), physical reactions (e.g., hypertension), and psychological reactions (e.g., frustration). Job dissatisfaction has been one of the most frequently studied psychological reactions. A relatively small number of possible job stressors have been studied by researchers. In this section, we will discuss how several of them relate to job satisfaction.

Workload

Workload is defined as demands placed on the employee by the job. Qualitative workload is the effort required by job tasks or the level of difficulty both mental and physical. Having to lift heavy objects and having to solve difficult mathematics problems both reflect qualitative workload. By contrast, quantitative workload is the amount of work that the employee must do.

Workload has been found to correlate with job dissatisfaction as well as other job strains (Jex & Beehr, 1991). However, correlations with job satisfaction have been inconsistent across studies. Dwyer and Ganster (1991) found in a sample of manufacturing employees that the correlation between workload and job satisfaction was .37, whereas Spector (1987) found a correlation of $-.27$ and $-.17$ with two different measures of global job satisfaction in a sample of clerical workers. Jamal (1990) found significant negative correlations of workload with job satisfaction, and Karasek, Gardell, and Lindell (1987) found that workload was negatively associated with job satisfaction and positively associated with heart disease. No significant correlation was found by Fox, Dwyer, and Ganster (1993) or Spector and O'Connell (1994). Unfortunately, it is not clear why results are inconsistent across these studies, although one possible explanation is that different measures of workload have been used in different studies.

Control

Control is the freedom that employees are given to make decisions about their work. Autonomy, which we discussed earlier, is a form of control limited to the employee's own job tasks. Control is a broader term that includes aspects of the organization that have little to do directly with an employee. Often, individuals are allowed to have input into broad policy issues that afford them an expanded sense

TABLE 4.4 Correlations of Job Satisfaction With Perceived Control From
Spector's (1986) Meta-Analysis

Facet	Number of Samples	Number of Participants	Mean Correlation
Global	61	21,096	.30
Coworkers	12	1,767	.19
Nature of work	30	5,764	.35
Pay	12	1,767	.19
Promotion	13	2,094	.20
Supervision	27	6,662	.34
Nature of work	30	5,764	.35

of control in the organization. Such control can have positive effects on a person's
job satisfaction.

Control is an important variable in the job stress process. It has been found to
correlate significantly with all three categories of job strains, especially psychological ones (Jex & Beehr, 1991). Spector (1986) conducted a meta-analysis
relating measures of perceived control with job satisfaction. The results are
summarized in Table 4.4, showing the mean correlations across studies of relations
between control and job satisfaction. As can be seen in the table, correlations are
largest for the intrinsic facets of growth and nature of work and smallest for
extrinsic facets of coworkers and pay.

The control studies included in Spector's (1986) meta-analysis assessed
perceived control. It is not clear that the correlations between control and job
satisfaction in these studies reflect the effects of the objective environment on
people. As noted previously in the discussion of job characteristics, reports about
the job can be affected by how an employee feels about that job (Spector, 1992a).

To get around this problem, we need studies that assess more objective
measures of control. Studies of machine pacing provide insights into how the actual
amount of control affects employees. For some tasks, the pace of work is determined by a machine rather than the employee. Machines often control the pace of
factory work, but computers have been pacing the work of an expanding number
of employees. Although the impact of machine pacing has not been well studied,
the limited research hints that it might have detrimental effects on people (e.g.,
Frankenhaeuser & Johansson, 1986). Smith, Hurrell, and Murphy (1981) compared postal workers who were machine paced with those in similar jobs who were
not. The machine-paced employees had lower job satisfaction.

The Demand/Control Model

The Demand/Control Model (Karasek, 1979) hypothesizes that control and job stressors interact in their effects on job strains, including job dissatisfaction. Demands are stressors such as workload that have the potential to induce strain in people. Control acts as a buffer to reduce the effects of demands. When an employee has high control, demands will have little relation with job strains. When the employee has little control, demands will be correlated with job strain. An important implication of this model is that the negative effects of demands can be reduced by increasing control.

Unfortunately, research support for the demand/control model has been inconsistent. Most studies have not found the expected interaction effect (Fletcher & Jones, 1993). An exception is Dwyer and Ganster (1991), who found an interaction of control and workload in the prediction of work satisfaction. However, the nature of their relation was not exactly consistent with the buffering effect. The lowest level of job satisfaction occurred for individuals who reported high control and low workload. The theory would predict that low control and high workload would produce the most dissatisfaction.

One of the problems with testing the demand/control model is that different studies have used different measures. The studies that used employee reports for all variables have tended not to find the expected interaction. Some of the studies that found the interaction have used more objective measures of control or demands (Dwyer & Ganster, 1991; Fox, Dwyer, & Ganster, 1993). The type of work performed is another possible factor in these studies. Westman (1992) found support for the model in a sample of clerks but not in a sample of managers.

Although the demand/control model is potentially important because of its implications for employee health and well-being, the lack of empirical support suggests that it may be an oversimplification. Fletcher and Jones (1993) argued for the addition of interpersonal support as an important factor in reducing job strains. Their results provide evidence that encouragement and support from others can be beneficial in increasing job satisfaction and reducing strains. Jex and Beehr (1991) noted that interpersonal conflict is an important stressor that has been practically neglected in the job stress domain.

Work Schedules

The standard work shift for most people is approximately 8 daylight hours per day for 5 weekdays each week. Nonstandard work schedules are spreading, requiring longer shifts and working different days and times. Increasingly, organizations are operating more than 8 hours per day, requiring extended hours for employees. At the same time, many employers are offering more flexibility in scheduling to accommodate individuals with families and other nonwork obligations. Of interest here will be four types of nonstandard work schedules: flexible work schedules, long work shifts, night shifts, and part-time work.

Flexible Work Schedules

Although fixed work schedules are still found in most organizations, increasingly employees are being offered more flexible arrangements. There are many varieties of flexible schedules ranging from those allowing complete freedom to work at any time to those that allow discretion only in limited ways, such as being able to begin the workday 1 or 2 hours late and quitting an equal amount of time late during the same day. The advantage to flexible schedules for the employer is that employees are encouraged to take care of personal business on their own time. Support for this notion is provided by studies that found that absence (Krausz & Freibach, 1983; Pierce & Newstrom, 1982) and tardiness (Ralston, 1989) are less with flexible work schedules.

The effects of flexible work schedules on job satisfaction have been somewhat inconsistent. Pierce and Newstrom (1982) and Ralston (1989) both found that job satisfaction was higher with flexible work schedules than with fixed work schedules. Limitations of both studies make conclusions somewhat tentative. Pierce and Newstrom compared two organizations, and it is possible that other factors accounted for the differences. Ralston used an indirect measure of job satisfaction, which is not entirely comparable with those used in other studies. No relation between work schedule and job satisfaction was found by Krausz and Freibach (1983), who compared employees of the same organization who did and did not have flexible work schedules. Perhaps over time these employees got used to the greater flexibility, and thus it did not relate to their job satisfaction. Although flexible work schedules might have positive effects on job satisfaction in at least some circumstances, more research is needed on this topic.

Long Shifts

Long shifts are those that exceed the standard of 8 hours per day. Organizations have experimented with 10- and 12-hour shifts, which have both advantages and disadvantages. The 10-hour shift allows for a 40-hour workweek to be compressed into 4 days. A 12-hour shift provides coverage of the entire 24-hour day with two full shifts rather than three required with 8-hour shifts.

The most frequently noted problem with long shifts is fatigue (Ronen & Primps, 1981). However, employees also like longer shifts because they can provide more days off (Breaugh, 1983). The availability of more usable free time can sometimes overcome fatigue, which is in large part a psychological reaction. Pierce and Dunham (1992) surveyed police officers who worked either 8- or 12-hour shifts. The 12-hour officers reported less fatigue, which might have been due to reduced feelings of stress resulting from having more free time.

The effects of long shifts on job satisfaction are usually positive. Although employees might experience more fatigue, they usually prefer long shifts and will enjoy increased job satisfaction if allowed to work fewer but longer days (Ronen & Primps, 1981). Results are not completely consistent across studies for either fatigue or job satisfaction results. It is likely that the nature of the job determines at least in part the effect of having to work long shifts.

A study that underscores the potentially adverse effects of working long hours was reported by Raggatt (1991). Raggatt investigated the effects of shift length on a sample of Australian bus drivers. Each driver drove a unique route that varied considerably in length, thus producing variation in shift length. A survey asked the drivers about job satisfaction, maladaptive behaviors (e.g., pill use), physical health problems, and psychological stress outcomes. Working excessive hours was associated with the following:

Alcohol consumption
Job dissatisfaction
Passenger complaints
Pill taking
Sleep disturbance

Job dissatisfaction was associated with all of these variables, as well as with the following:

Accidents
Doctor visits
Frequent speeding
Health complaints
Psychological symptoms of stress

A model was developed that presented a multistage process in which having to work long hours leads to maladaptive behavior (e.g., alcohol and pill use) as well as sleep disturbance, which leads to job dissatisfaction and other job strains. Clearly, for some jobs long shifts are not a good idea.

Night Shifts

Many organizations, such as hospitals and police departments, operate 24 hours per day requiring two or three shifts of workers to cover the entire time. Many employers have employees rotate shifts so that each individual will take turns working days, evenings, and nights. Both working at night and rotating shifts have been researched. These practices have been found to have detrimental affects on at least some employees.

The biggest problem with night work is that the typical cycle of sleep/waking is disturbed. Circadian rhythms of physiological events occur regularly throughout the day. These include changes in body temperature and in bloodstream hormone levels. Disruption of these cycles by working when the individual would normally be sleeping can lead to health problems.

The most frequent health problem associated with night shift work is sleep disturbance. People who work at night are more likely to have problems with sleeping than their day shift counterparts (e.g., Barton & Folkard, 1991; Koller, Kundi, & Cervinka, 1978). Koller et al. also found that night shift workers were more likely to have digestive problems than day workers. This may be due at least in part to the secretion of digestive hormones, which is lower at night than during the day (Akerstedt & Theorell, 1976).

Both Barton and Folkard (1991) and Jamal and Baba (1992) found that the adverse effects of night shift work might be due more to shift rotation than to night work itself. In both studies, people on permanent night shifts were compared to people who were working nights temporarily because of shift rotation. Barton and Folkard found that the adverse effects of night work on sleep did not occur for employees on permanent night shifts. Of more interest to our present discussion is the relation of shift work to job satisfaction in Jamal and Baba's study. Employees who were assigned to temporary night shifts had lower job satisfaction than individuals who worked permanent night shifts. Thus working nights itself does not seem to affect job satisfaction, but rotating from day shift to night shift might have a detrimental effect on employee feelings about the job.

Part-Time Work

Increasingly organizations are hiring people to work fewer than the more or less standard 40-hour week. Some of the motivation for this practice is that part-timers do not have to be given the same benefits, such as medical insurance, which adds substantial costs over and above pay. Because part-time employees do not get the same rewards, even when they do the same work, one might hypothesize that their job satisfaction would be lower than the job satisfaction of full-time employees. Interestingly, this does not always seem to be the case.

Eberhardt and Shani (1984) compared part-time and full-time female and male hospital employees on their overall job satisfaction. The part-timers were more satisfied with their jobs than the full-timers. In a similar comparison, Jackofsky and Peters (1987) reported that part-time employees of a retail sales organization had higher job satisfaction than their full-time counterparts. Although these two studies found that part-timers were more satisfied than full-timers, this has not been the case in other studies (Feldman, 1990; Miller & Terborg, 1979). Barling and Gallagher (1996) reviewed the existing research and concluded that although global job satisfaction is often equivalent, part-timers may be less satisfied with rewards and more satisfied with social aspects of the job, for example, coworkers or supervision. Feldman (1990) noted that the underlying causes of job satisfaction might be different for full-time and part-time employees. For example, many part-time employees are students who consider the job to be temporary. Schedule flexibility to minimize conflict with class schedules might be more important than benefits and rewards. Unfortunately, there has been insufficient research conducted on part-time employees to be able to understand how their reactions differ from full-timers.

Personal Antecedents of Job Satisfaction

Although the importance of individual differences to the experience of job satisfaction was recognized as far back as the Hawthorne studies of the 1920s, the environmental perspective has dominated the research and theory in this domain. In the mid-1980s, there was increased interest in personality effects on job satisfaction. Studies have provided convincing evidence that personality is clearly a factor. In fact, some researchers have argued that there may be genetic predispositions to like or dislike the job (Arvey, Bouchard, Segal, & Abraham, 1989).

In their writings about the Hawthorne studies, the researchers noted that certain individuals were chronically unhappy about their jobs (Roethlisberger, 1941). They called them the chronic kickers in recognition of their constant complaints. More recently, Schneider and Dachler (1978) noticed in a longitudinal study that when they assessed job satisfaction repeatedly over time, it was remarkably stable. This observation led them to speculate that job satisfaction was caused in part by an employee's personality rather than just the job.

Staw and Ross (1985) followed up on the job satisfaction consistency idea and assessed job satisfaction in people who changed employers and/or job type. Their results were that job satisfaction was relatively stable in people who changed jobs. People who liked one job were likely to like another job. Staw and Ross concluded that job satisfaction was in part due to personality. Some people are predisposed to like their jobs, whereas others are not.

Other researchers have replicated Staw and Ross's findings that job satisfaction assessments correlate across jobs (Gerhart, 1987; Gupta, Jenkins, & Beehr, 1992). Newton and Keenan (1991) showed how both environment and person can be important. They repeatedly surveyed a group of British engineers during their first 4 years of employment after college graduation. Although job satisfaction correlated across jobs, it also tended to increase when the individual started a new job. This study suggests that some people are inclined to be more satisfied with their jobs than others because of their underlying personality, but job changes still lead to increased job satisfaction.

Although this job satisfaction consistency research seems quite compelling, it has had its critics. Davis-Blake and Pfeffer (1989) argued that job satisfaction can be stable across jobs for reasons other than personality. It is possible that certain individuals tend to choose good jobs, whereas others do not. Thus, the observed consistency in job satisfaction would be attributable to the job rather than the person.

In a 50-year lifespan longitudinal study, Staw, Bell, and Clausen (1986) provided stronger evidence than the consistency studies for the role of individual factors in job satisfaction. Staw et al. had available data from the intergenerational studies begun at the University of California, Berkeley, during the 1920s. Adolescents in this study were assessed using interviews, and follow-up questionnaires were given several times during their lives. The extensive material for each participant from adolescence was reviewed by clinicians who rated them on several personality traits, which were distilled into a single affective disposition score. Affective disposition in adolescence was found to significantly correlate with job satisfaction measured up to 50 years later. Clearly, there are factors within the individual that contribute to their job satisfaction.

Evidence for a genetic component to this consistency of job satisfaction comes from a study by Arvey et al. (1989). They surveyed a group of identical twins who were reared separately and found that their job satisfaction was correlated. From the magnitude of relation, it was estimated that about 30% of the variance in job satisfaction is attributable to genetic factors. In other words, if one member of the twin was satisfied with his or her job, the corresponding member was likely to feel the same about work. This is compelling evidence that there is some genetic component to job satisfaction, although the nature of the underlying process is unknown. It seems likely that some individuals are predisposed to be happier in life, and this can affect job attitudes.

Personality Traits and Job Satisfaction

The above-mentioned studies have demonstrated that job satisfaction has a personality component, but they fail to give much insight into the nature of the traits that lead to job satisfaction (Judge, 1992). Studies of particular personality traits offer clues about how personality affects job satisfaction. Although many traits have been shown to correlate significantly with job satisfaction, most research with personality has done little more than demonstrate relations without offering much theoretical explanation. Two traits in particular have been given extensive attention beyond just demonstrating significant correlations with job satisfaction. Locus of control and negative affectivity seem to play a role in the development of job satisfaction.

Locus of Control

Locus of control is a cognitive variable that represents an individual's gener-alized belief in his or her ability to control positive and negative reinforcements in life. An external believes in control by outside forces or people. An internal believes that he or she is able to influence reinforcements. Beliefs about control of reinforcements can have an effect on work attitudes.

There have been many studies that have found a significant correlation of locus of control with many work variables. For example, locus of control relates to job performance, leadership behavior, perceptions of the job, and work motiva-tion. It also correlates significantly with job satisfaction (O'Brien, 1983; Spector,

1982). In these studies, the more internal a person scores, the higher his or her job satisfaction tends to be.

Most locus of control research has used general measures, such as Rotter's (1966), which assesses how a person tends to feel across all domains of life. However, domain specific measures are available that assess how a person feels about a particular aspect of life. For the work domain, Spector (1988) developed the Work Locus of Control Scale to assess how people feel concerning control of reinforcements only in the workplace. This scale has been shown to correlate with job satisfaction (Moyle, 1995; Sargent & Terry, 1994), often at a higher level than does general locus of control (Spector, 1988). In a longitudinal study, Spector and O'Connell (1994) found that locus of control assessed in college significantly correlated with job satisfaction measured on the job more than a year later. Like Staw et al.'s (1986) study, personality was shown to have an impact on job satisfaction later in life.

Several mechanisms might account for the relation of locus of control and job satisfaction. Spector (1982) hypothesized that the relation between these two variables might be mediated by job performance. He noted that internals tend to perform their jobs better than externals, and if job performance is associated with rewards, satisfaction with the job might result. Thus, internals have higher job satisfaction because they benefit from the rewards of their better job performance. Waddell (1983) found locus of control differences among women in different occupations. It is possible that externals are in worse jobs than internals, thus accounting for job satisfaction differences.

Negative Affectivity

Negative affectivity or NA is a personality variable that reflects a person's tendency to experience negative emotions, such as anxiety or depression, across a wide variety of situations. Watson, Pennebaker, and Folger (1986) hypothesized that people who are high in NA would experience the job in universally negative ways, which would result in low job satisfaction. Research has consistently found that measures of negative emotions correlate negatively with job satisfaction. People who are high in NA tend to be low in job satisfaction (e.g., Brief, Burke, George, Robinson, & Webster, 1988; Cropanzano, James, & Konovsky, 1993; Judge, 1993; Schaubroeck, Ganster, & Fox, 1992; Schaubroeck, Ganster, & Kemmerer, 1994).

As with locus of control, it is important to understand why NA correlates with job satisfaction. Several mechanisms have been suggested. Moyle (1995) hypothesized that high-NA people may experience higher levels of all sorts of negative affect at work, including job dissatisfaction. She gave an alternative explanation that people who are high in NA tend to perceive their job situation as being negative, which leads them to experience job dissatisfaction. Schaubroeck et al. (1994) speculated that low-NA people make better job choices and have higher levels of job satisfaction because they are in better jobs. Watson et al. (1986) felt that NA contaminates many organizational measures, including measures of job satisfaction. They suggested that correlations between job satisfaction and other organizational variables assessed through employee questionnaires were due to the influence of NA on responses to surveys. Recent research on this possibility finds little support that NA is the explanation for correlations of organizational variables with job satisfaction (e.g., Moyle, 1995; Williams, Gavin, & Williams, 1996).

Person-Job Fit

Most of the research discussed in this book so far has tended to investigate characteristics of the job and characteristics of the person separately. Some research has looked at the interaction between job and person factors to see if certain types of people respond differently to certain types of jobs. This person-job fit approach posits that there will be job satisfaction when characteristics of the job are matched to characteristics of the person (Edwards, 1991). One such idea is contained in the job characteristics theory (Hackman & Oldham, 1976), which hypothesized a role for growth need strength.

One stream of research that has taken the person-job fit perspective has looked at the discrepancy between what a person says he or she wants on the job and what he or she has. For example, a person might be asked how much skill variety there is on the job versus how much skill variety is wanted. The smaller the discrepancy, the higher should be the job satisfaction. Studies that have used this procedure have generally found that discrepancy relates to job satisfaction as expected (Edwards, 1991).

A different approach has been taken in many of the job characteristics studies that investigated the hypothesized role of growth need strength or GNS. Note that a moderator is a variable that affects the relation among other variables. In job characteristics studies, growth need strength is treated as a moderator of the relation between job characteristics and job satisfaction; that is, people high in GNS will respond favorably to a high-scope job, whereas their counterparts who are low in GNS will not. In their meta-analysis, Loher et al. (1985) found support for the moderator effect. The correlation between job characteristics and job satisfaction was higher for individuals high on GNS than for individuals low on GNS.

Moderator effects with other personality variables related to other work variables have been more elusive. For example, Moyle (1995) was unable to find a moderator effect for NA on the relation between job stressors and job satisfaction. She did, however, find one for a measure of psychological well-being. Jex and Gudanowski (1992) also failed to find a significant moderator effect of self-efficacy (the tendency to see oneself as competent) on the relation between role ambiguity and job satisfaction, and constraints and job satisfaction.

5

Potential Effects of Job Satisfaction

There are many behaviors and employee outcomes that have been hypothesized to be the result of job satisfaction or dissatisfaction. These include not
only work variables such as job performance and turnover but also nonwork
variables such as health and life satisfaction. Many of these hypothesized effects
of job satisfaction have been shown to correlate with it. However, it has yet to be
established that the relations are in fact causal. For this reason, this chapter's title
contains the word *potential.*

Job Performance

Conventional wisdom says that job satisfaction should be related to job
performance. After all, a happy employee should be a productive employee.

Studies have established that the correlation between these two variables is rather modest. Two meta-analyses found that the mean correlation of job performance with global job satisfaction was approximately .25 (Iaffaldano & Muchinsky, 1985; Petty, McGee, & Cavender, 1984). The correlation with individual facets varied in the Iaffaldano and Muchinsky meta-analysis from .054 with pay satisfaction to .196 for nature of work satisfaction.

The magnitude of correlation between job performance and job satisfaction is unexpectedly low. However, it should be considered to be a conservative lower bound estimate in light of problems with job performance measures. Supervisor ratings have been used in most studies as the job performance measure. They suffer from rating biases and restriction of range, both of which reduce correlations with other variables. Better performance measures would be expected to result in stronger correlations.

The above-mentioned meta-analyses established that job performance and job satisfaction correlate with one another, at least to a moderate extent. However, they do little to explain the reasons for observed correlations. Although it is possible that job satisfaction leads to job performance, the opposite direction of causality is also equally feasible. People who are happy with their jobs might be more motivated, work harder, and therefore perform better. There is stronger evidence that people who perform better like their jobs better because of the rewards that are often associated with good performance.

Evidence exists for the hypothesis that job satisfaction is the result of good job performance. Jacobs and Solomon (1977) hypothesized that the correlation between job satisfaction and job performance would be higher in jobs where good performance was rewarded than in jobs where it was not. Under such conditions, employees who perform well get rewards, and rewards should lead to job satisfaction. Consistent with their predictions, Jacobs and Solomon found that job performance and job satisfaction were more strongly correlated when organizations tied rewards to good job performance.

Caldwell and O'Reilly (1990) provided indirect evidence that job performance can lead to job satisfaction. They showed that matching employee abilities to job requirements enhances job performance. They also found that matching employee abilities to job requirements enhances job satisfaction, as well. People who are better able to do their jobs well and perform well tend to have higher job satisfaction. It seems likely that job satisfaction is caused by job performance, although this relation might be explained by the rewards given to individuals who perform well.

Organizational Citizenship Behavior (OCB)

Organizational citizenship behavior or OCB is behavior by an employee intended to help coworkers or the organization. In contrast to job performance, OCB is behavior that goes beyond the formal requirements of a job (Schnake, 1991). It consists of those voluntary things employees do to help their coworkers and employers. What makes such behavior OCB is that it is not part of the individual's assigned responsibilities. Schnake provided the following OCB examples:

Being punctual
Helping others
Making suggestions to improve things
Not wasting time at work

Organ and Konovsky (1989) categorized OCB into two types:

1. Altruism
2. Compliance

Altruism is behavior that helps other people. Helping others and making suggestions would be examples. Compliance is doing what is required on the job without having to be closely monitored and reminded. Being punctual and not wasting time are examples.

OCB is usually assessed with scales completed by the supervisors of the target person being studied. Perhaps the most frequently used scale was developed by Smith, Organ, and Near (1983). It contains both altruism and compliance items. Sample items can be seen in Table 5.1.

Conventional wisdom suggests that job satisfaction should lead to job performance. As discussed earlier, little evidence exists that this is true. Rather it seems that job performance might lead to job satisfaction when job performance leads to rewards. However, it could be that job satisfaction leads to OCB rather than required performance. People who are happy with their jobs might be willing to go beyond what is required of them. Evidence exists that supervisors clearly distinguish OCB from required job performance in that their ratings of both are only slightly correlated (MacKenzie, Podsakoff, & Fetter, 1991).

Schnake (1991) hypothesized that OCB is caused by good treatment from the supervisor and by job satisfaction. In fact, job satisfaction and OCB have been

TABLE 5.1 Four Items From the Organizational Citizenship Behavior Scale

Assists supervisor with his or her work
Makes innovative suggestions to improve department
Punctuality
Gives advance notice if unable to come to work

SOURCE: Organ and Konovsky (1989).

found to intercorrelate (e.g., Becker & Billings, 1993; Farh, Podsakoff, & Organ, 1990). Organ and Ryan (1995) conducted a meta-analysis of OCB studies. They computed separate mean correlations for the two types of OCB—altruism and compliance—which were .24 (28 studies), and .22 (25 studies), respectively. These correlations are similar to those from the meta-analyses for general job perform-ance. Similar findings have been reported from quite diverse countries, including Nigeria (Munene, 1995) and Taiwan (Farh et al., 1990). Of course, correlation alone does not establish a causal link, so further research will be needed to demonstrate that OCB is the result of job satisfaction.

McNeely and Meglino (1994) divided OCB behavior into actions that benefit individuals versus actions that benefit organizations. Both types of OCB correlated significantly with job satisfaction at about the same level ($r = .26$ for individual benefit and $r = .25$ for organizational benefit). Furthermore, they found that each OCB type had different potential antecedents. Individual benefit was significantly correlated with concern for others and empathy, whereas organizational benefit was significantly correlated with perceptions of equity at work and desire for recognition. The authors concluded that for individual benefit OCB, personal factors were important with job satisfaction also contributing to the decision to help others. For organizational OCB, organizational factors, such as perceptions of equity, led to job satisfaction, which affected the decision to help the organiza-tion. Individuals who perceived fairness in rewards at work would experience job satisfaction, which would lead to OCB. These ideas make conceptual sense but need confirmation with additional research.

Withdrawal Behavior

Many theories hypothesize that people who dislike their jobs will avoid them, either permanently by quitting or temporarily by being absent or coming in late.

These withdrawal behaviors have been given more attention than any other in job satisfaction research. Job satisfaction is a central variable in almost every theory of withdrawal behavior. Mitra, Jenkins, and Gupta (1992) noted that many researchers consider absence and turnover to be related phenomena that have the same underlying motivations to escape a dissatisfying job.

In a meta-analysis Mitra et al. found that absence and turnover tended to be intercorrelated. Employees who quit a job were likely to have had higher levels of absence just prior to leaving the job than did employees who did not quit. However, this relation does not necessarily mean that absence and turnover are alternative reactions to job dissatisfaction. On many jobs, people lose their pool of sick leave on leaving, which might motivate someone about to quit a job to consume their sick leave rather than lose it. They might also be absent because of job interviews preceding their quitting. Reasons for missing work might be quite different for employees who do not quit.

Absence

Absence is a phenomenon that can reduce organizational effectiveness and efficiency by increasing labor costs. On many jobs, floaters or substitutes are required for each absent employee. The employee might continue to get paid, resulting in increased costs to pay substitutes. Where absence rates among employees is high, the costs can be quite high. Not surprisingly, organizations are concerned about absence.

Theories of absence hypothesize that job satisfaction plays a critical role in an employee's decision to be absent (Steers & Rhodes, 1978). People who dislike their jobs should be expected to avoid coming to work. However, empirical support for this position has been surprisingly difficult to find. Correlations between job satisfaction and absence have been inconsistent across studies.

Mean correlations found in meta-analyses have been quite small for both facet and global job satisfaction. For example, Farrell and Stamm (1988) found mean correlations in their meta-analysis of −.13 and −.10 with two different measures of absence. Scott and Taylor (1985) compiled results from 114 studies and found a mean correlation between job satisfaction and absence of only −.15. Hackett and Guion (1985) found larger correlations for some facets than others, although the strongest was still only −.11 for nature of work.

Although correlations between job satisfaction and absence are usually quite small, occasionally researchers have found correlations that are larger. For example, Tharenou (1993) found a −.34 correlation in her study. She used complex statistical procedures to test for the direction of causality. Interestingly, her results suggested that absence that is under the employee's control might cause job satisfaction rather than the opposite. Her explanation is that people who are absent make negative attributions about their employers to justify their behavior. In other words, to rationalize being absent, a person might focus on negative aspects of work, such as unfair treatment. This could affect job satisfaction in a negative way.

At least one statistical reason for the small correlations between job satisfaction and absence is the distribution of absences across employees (Hammer & Landau, 1981). In most samples, the distribution of absences is extremely skewed, with few employees having many instances of absence. A typical absence distribution from a sample of employees is shown in Figure 5.1. The severe nonnormality of absence distributions can attenuate correlations. Hammer and Landau note that correlation might not be the best statistic to use for absence data, because the required assumptions of normally distributed observations are too badly violated. This means that the correlation coefficient is difficult to interpret, requiring the use of other data analysis techniques.

It seems likely that the correlation between job satisfaction and absence is not bigger because absence is a complex variable that can have multiple causes (Kohler & Mathieu, 1993). A person might be absent because of being ill, a family member's being ill, being fatigued, or having to conduct personal business, as well as just not wanting to go to work. The first four reasons might or might not have anything to do with job satisfaction. Clearly, the reason for absence should be considered if we are going to understand the role of job satisfaction.

Dalton and Mesch (1991) demonstrated that the reasons for absence influenced its correlates. They classified absence into absence due to illness versus absence due to other causes. They then correlated the two types with several variables. Absence due to illness was significantly correlated with job satisfaction, but absence due to other causes was not. It was related to absence policies and tenure. The less restrictive the policy and the longer the tenure, the more absence.

Job satisfaction may have played a central role in research on absence, but it has been replaced in recent years by other more important variables. For example, Goff, Mount, and Jamison (1990) found that having primary child care responsibilities predicted absence much better than did job satisfaction. Having to take care of children is a reason for absence that is more important than disliking the job. Haccoun and Jeanrie (1995) reported larger correlations (as high as .37) between absence and attitudes tolerant of absence than are typically found for job satisfaction.

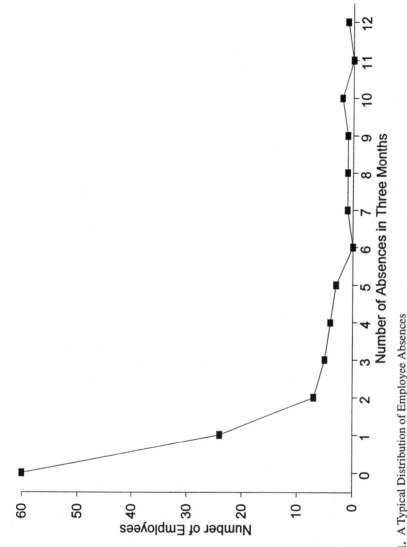

Figure 5.1. A Typical Distribution of Employee Absences
SOURCE: From author's unpublished data set.

Farrell and Stamm (1988) found in their meta-analysis of 72 studies that the two best correlates of absence were prior history of absence and organizational absence control policies, with mean correlations of .47 and –.30, respectively. Organizations that have lax absence policies will have more absences, especially from individuals who have tendencies to stay home from work.

One additional factor that may lead to absence is what Nicholson and Johns (1985) have called the absence culture of an organization or work group. When norms of a group support absence, there will be high levels. Conversely, when the norms of the group discourage absence, there will be low levels. Several studies support the idea that organizations have cultures that determine absence. For example, Mathieu and Kohler (1990) found that individuals tended to have more absences if they were in work groups where members were absent frequently rather than rarely. Harrison and Shaffer (1993) found that an employee's estimate of coworkers' number of absences significantly predicted the number of absences by the employee. Finally, Martocchio (1994) showed that coworker reports of absence costs and benefits predicted the absences of individuals. These studies suggest that the decision not to come to work is affected by the individual's knowledge about coworker's absence behavior.

Turnover

Most theories of turnover view it as the result of employee job dissatisfaction (e.g., Bluedorn, 1982; Mobley, Griffeth, Hand, & Meglino, 1979). People who dislike their jobs will try to find alternative employment. Studies have been reasonably consistent in showing a correlation between job satisfaction and turnover (e.g., Crampton & Wagner, 1994; Hulin, Roznowski, & Hachiya, 1985). Furthermore, it seems certain that this correlation is causal—job dissatisfaction leads to turnover.

The reason for certainty about the causal effects of job satisfaction on employee turnover is because longitudinal designs are usually applied in these studies. Job satisfaction is measured in a sample of employees at one point in time. At a later time, perhaps a year later, the researcher determines who has quit. Job satisfaction levels are compared between those who quit and those who did not. It is clear with this design that causality must run from job satisfaction to turnover rather than the reverse because the behavior did not occur until months or in some cases years after the job satisfaction assessment.

Models of turnover place job satisfaction in the center of a complex process that involves factors both inside and outside of the employing organization. Figure

5.2 is a simplified model that shows how this process might work. Characteristics of the individual combine with characteristics of the job environment in determining level of job satisfaction. If the job satisfaction level is sufficiently low, the person will develop a behavioral intention to quit the job. That intention may lead to job search activities, which if successful will lead to turnover. Alternate employment opportunities are important because a person is not likely to quit without another job offer.

There is good research support for the connections among the variables in Figure 5.2. The causes of job satisfaction itself were discussed in the prior chapter. Both employee and workplace factors have been found to result jointly in job satisfaction. Job satisfaction correlates quite well with intention of quitting the job (e.g., Blau, 1993; Shore, Newton, & Thornton, 1990). In a meta-analysis, Tett and Meyer (1993) found a mean correlation of $-.58$ between job satisfaction and intention.

Furthermore, Blau found that intention to quit related to job search behaviors ($r = .27, .25$ in two samples), such as these:

Contacted an employment agency
Prepared or revised a résumé
Sent résumés to employers
Went on a job interview

Finally, Blau showed that these behaviors were the strongest predictor of subsequent turnover, with a correlation of .43 and .41 in two samples. By contrast, the correlations in his samples between job satisfaction and turnover were only $-.16$ and $-.15$, which are not far from the mean of $-.25$ found by Tett and Meyer (1993) in their meta-analysis.

The importance of alternate employment opportunities has been indirectly demonstrated in studies that assessed labor market factors in relation to turnover. It has been found that unemployment rate correlates strongly with quit rate in organizations (Carsten & Spector, 1987). In two investigations of the effects of unemployment, it was found that labor market factors interact with job satisfaction in predicting quitting (Carsten & Spector, 1987; Gerhart, 1990). In these studies, it was shown that job dissatisfaction was related more strongly with turnover during periods when the rate of unemployment was low than when the rate of unemployment was high. The explanation is that dissatisfied employees who wish to quit can do so only when it is possible to find an alternative job.

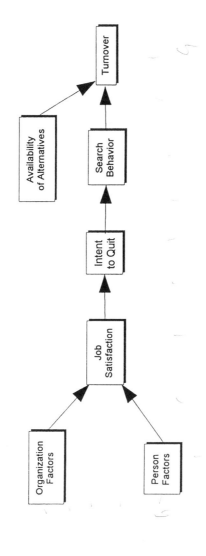

Figure 5.2. Model of Employee Turnover as a Function of Job Satisfaction and Unemployment Rate

Mitra et al. (1992) conducted a meta-analysis in which they demonstrated the same effect of unemployment on the turnover–absence correlation across studies. They determined the unemployment rates for the times during which data were collected in studies. They found that correlation coefficients tended to be higher when data were collected during times of low unemployment than during periods of high unemployment. Apparently, absence and turnover are related to one another more strongly during periods when it is relatively easy to find alternative employment.

So far turnover has been approached as a reaction by individuals to the work environment. Judge (1993) hypothesized that the affective disposition of the individual would interact with job satisfaction in influencing decisions to quit the job. On the basis of the work of Weitz (1952), he hypothesized that people with positive affective tendencies that were reflected in a general tendency to be satisfied in life would have a more difficult time handling a dissatisfying job and would be more likely to quit than would someone who was more used to being in a dissatisfied and negative emotional state. He administered scales of affective disposition (Weitz, 1952) and job satisfaction. He later determined which employees had quit. Consistent with predictions, the highest turnover rates were for people who had favorable dispositions in general but who disliked their current jobs, whereas the lowest turnover rates were for people with favorable dispositions and high job satisfaction (turnover rates were approximately 32% versus 6%, respectively). For individuals with unfavorable dispositions, rates ranged from about 15% to 10%. The results of this study underscore how characteristics of the employee interact with characteristics of the organization in determining behavior.

Burnout

Burnout is a distressed emotional/psychological state experienced on the job. Where job satisfaction is an attitudinal response, burnout is more of an emotional response to the job. Burnout theory proposes that a person who is in a state of burnout experiences symptoms of emotional exhaustion and low work motivation, not unlike depression. The work on burnout originally came from research on direct care employees, such as nurses or social workers. It was felt by early burnout researchers that providing direct care to people in need led to symptoms of burnout not likely to be experienced by employees in other types of work. In recent years, burnout research has been conducted with many types of jobs that do not involve direct care of people.

According to Maslach and Jackson (1981), there are three components of burnout. Depersonalization is the emotional distancing from direct care clients that results in a callous and uncaring attitude toward others. Emotional exhaustion is the feeling of fatigue and lack of enthusiasm for work. Reduced personal accomplishment is the sense that nothing of value is being done at work by the person.

As might be expected, burnout correlates significantly with job satisfaction in that dissatisfied employees are likely to report high levels of burnout (e.g., Bacharach, Bamberger, & Conley, 1991; Shirom, 1989). Lee and Ashforth (1993) found stronger relations between job satisfaction and emotional exhaustion ($r = -.50$) than with depersonalization ($r = -.33$) or personal accomplishment ($r = .28$). Note that personal accomplishment is scored so that low scores reflect high burnout, which is different from the other burnout dimensions. Burnout also correlates significantly with many variables that are correlates of job satisfaction (Cordes & Dougherty, 1993). For example, high burnout levels have been associated with low levels of control and life satisfaction and with high levels of health symptoms and intention of quitting the job (Lee & Ashforth, 1993; Shirom, 1989).

A model of burnout was developed by Lee and Ashforth (1993) that hypothesized a causal chain from job conditions to job satisfaction to burnout. They explained that emotional exhaustion is a reaction to the negative feelings a person has when in a dissatisfying job. The other components of burnout follow from emotional exhaustion. Using complex statistical procedures of structural equation modeling, Lee and Ashforth found support for their model.

Physical Health and Psychological Well-Being

Concerns have been raised that both physical and psychological health might be influenced by job attitudes. Individuals who dislike their jobs could experience adverse health outcomes. These outcomes include both physical symptoms and psychological problems. It has also been suggested that job dissatisfaction results in a shortened lifespan (Palmore, 1969). If true, this makes the optimization of job satisfaction an important social priority.

Many correlational studies have shown a link between health and job satisfaction. For example, researchers have reported significant correlations between job satisfaction and physical or psychosomatic symptoms, such as headache and upset stomach (e.g., Begley & Czajka, 1993; Fox, Dwyer, & Ganster, 1993; Lee, Ashford, & Bobko, 1990; O'Driscoll & Beehr, 1994). Job dissatisfaction has also been found to be associated with emotional states of anxiety (Jex & Gudanowski,

1992; Spector et al., 1988) and depression (Bluen, Barling, & Burns, 1990; Schaubroeck et al., 1992). Attempts to link job satisfaction to more direct physiological measures of health have been less fruitful. For example, Ganster and colleagues found only 1 of 11 significant correlations of various physiological measures ($r = -.13$ for palmar sweat with job satisfaction). Blood pressure and catecholamine (adrenaline) levels were not correlated significantly with job satisfaction.

Some hints about how people's job attitudes could influence their physiology comes from job stress research done in Sweden (Johansson, 1981). This researcher assessed catecholamine levels as people worked on machine-paced and self-paced jobs. The results showed that catecholamines associated with negative emotions increased when people did machine-paced jobs, and decreased when they did self-paced jobs. The researchers speculated that performing jobs that caused distress led to increases in certain catecholamines. It seems reasonable to speculate that being in a dissatisfying job would have a similar effect.

Although it has been well established in the literature that job satisfaction relates to physical symptoms, complications for interpretation of correlations are caused by the nature of research designs in most studies. The self-reports of both job satisfaction and symptoms have been hypothesized to be the result of affective dispositions (Brief et al., 1988; Watson et al., 1986). This position is that people who are high in negative affectivity will tend to be dissatisfied with work and experience frequent physical symptoms. The relation between these variables is attributable to the individual's personality rather than effects of job satisfaction on physical symptoms.

There has been enough connection found between job satisfaction and both physical and psychological health to produce concern. Even though much of the evidence is circumstantial, it seems likely that job experiences affect health. Job dissatisfaction can be an indicator that something is wrong for an individual at work. Of course, the causes of the employee's distress might have little to do with the job. However, years spent in an unhappy work situation have the potential to adversely affect physical and psychological health.

Counterproductive Behavior

The opposite of organizational citizenship behavior is counterproductive behavior. It consists of acts committed by an employee that either intentionally or unintentionally hurt the organization. This includes aggression against coworkers, aggression against the employer, sabotage, and theft. These behaviors have many causes, but often, they are associated with dissatisfaction and frustration at work.

Only a handful of studies have investigated causes of counterproductive behavior at work. Chen and Spector (1992) found that job satisfaction correlated significantly with employee reports of engaging in aggression against others, hostility toward others, sabotage, and theft at work. Keenan and Newton (1984) likewise found a relation between experiencing feelings of hostility at work and job satisfaction. Dissatisfied employees are more likely than their satisfied counterparts to engage in all of these behaviors.

Counterproductive behaviors are not the typical reaction to job dissatisfaction, although they occur frequently enough to be of great concern. An important factor involved in these behaviors is control at work. Individuals who believe they have control at work are less likely to commit these acts than individuals who believe they have no control (Spector, 1997). Perlow and Latham (1993) found that locus of control predicted abuse of clients by employees of a residential care facility for mentally retarded individuals. Abusive behavior was more likely for employees with an external rather than internal locus of control. Storms and Spector (1987) reported that locus of control moderated the relation of frustration at work with aggression, hostility toward others, and sabotage. Externals but not internals showed a relation between feelings of frustration and reports of counterproductive behavior.

Although little research has been reported on counterproductive behavior, the few available studies clearly suggest an important role for job satisfaction. Anything that an organization can do to make the workplace better for its employees has the potential of enhancing job satisfaction and reducing counterproductive behavior. Organizational constraints would be particularly important because they seem to be closely tied to frustration at work (Spector, 1997). Often, actions as simple as offering reasonable explanations to employees for decisions can help reduce counterproductive behaviors (Greenberg, 1990). Of course, there are individual differences in the tendency for people to engage in counterproductive behavior (Perlow & Latham, 1993), so that changing the job will not likely eliminate the problem completely.

Life Satisfaction

The interplay of work and nonwork is an important ingredient in understanding people's reactions to jobs. We tend to study work mainly in the workplace,

TABLE 5.2 Percentage of People in 18 Countries Who Report Being
Satisfied With Life

Country	Percentage Satisfied
Iceland	87
Canada	86
Germany	84
United States	83
Thailand	80
United Kingdom	66
Chile	65
France	64
Costa Rica	63
Venezuela	62
Japan	60
Dominican Republic	52
India	52
China	51
Taiwan	42
Spain	41
Mexico	36
Hungary	21

SOURCE: Gallup Organization (1995).

but employees are influenced by events and situations outside of their place of work. Conversely, behavior and feelings about nonwork are influenced by experience on the job. Life satisfaction refers to a person's feelings about life in general. It can be assessed on the facet level as satisfaction with specific areas of life, such as family or recreation. It can also be assessed globally, as overall satisfaction with life. Because life satisfaction reflects overall feelings about life, it is considered a measure of emotional well-being.

In the 1991 Gallup poll concerning job satisfaction, questions were also asked about life satisfaction. The majority of Americans in that poll, 87%, reported that they were generally satisfied with life (Hugick & Leonard, 1991). In a 1995 Gallup poll of 18 countries, 83% of Americans reported being satisfied with their lives (see Table 5.2). The most satisfied citizens were in Iceland and Canada, and the least satisfied were in Hungary and Mexico.

Because work is a major component of life for people who are employed, it seems obvious that job satisfaction and life satisfaction should be related. Three hypotheses have been discussed about how job and life satisfaction are related (Rain, Lane, & Steiner, 1991). The spillover hypothesis suggests that feelings in one area of life affect feelings in other areas. A person who is satisfied on the job is likely to be satisfied with life in general (Weaver, 1978). The compensation hypothesis states that people will compensate for dissatisfaction in one area of life by cultivating satisfaction in another. A person with a dissatisfying job will put the majority of his or her energy into nonwork activities, whereas someone with a dissatisfying nonwork life may put the majority of his or her effort into work. The segmentation hypothesis posits that people compartmentalize their lives, making work and nonwork separate.

The spillover hypothesis predicts a positive correlation between job satisfaction and life satisfaction. Feelings in one area of life affect others, resulting in positive relations between the two satisfactions. The compensation hypothesis predicts the opposite. A person who is dissatisfied in one area will be satisfied in others. The segmentation hypothesis predicts no relation. People will keep different areas of life separate so that job satisfaction and life satisfaction will be uncorrelated.

The research findings in this domain clearly favor the spillover hypothesis. Studies consistently find that job satisfaction and life satisfaction are moderately and positively correlated (e.g., Judge & Watanabe, 1993; Lance, Lautenschlager, Sloan, & Varca, 1989; Schaubroeck et al., 1992; Weaver, 1978). Lance et al. (1989) found a correlation of .58 between job and life satisfaction. Facet satisfactions for marital and social activity domains were also correlated with job satisfaction.

The correlation between job satisfaction and life satisfaction alone does not offer much insight into which might cause which. It is possible that job satisfaction causes life satisfaction, or the reverse. A longitudinal study by Judge and Watanabe (1993) using complex statistical procedures of structural equation modeling provided evidence that both directions of causality are likely. That is, each type of satisfaction affects the other. Likewise, support for the spillover hypothesis was found with a representative, national sample of executives in the United States (Judge, Boudreau, & Bretz, 1993). Structural equation modeling of their responses to job and life satisfaction measures suggested that each is a likely cause of the other.

6

Concluding Remarks

This book has briefly summarized the vast literature on job satisfaction. It covered assessment of job satisfaction, how people generally feel about work, possible causes, and potential effects of this important work variable. The size of this literature makes any overview an ambitious undertaking. Locke (1976) estimated that by 1972, 3,350 job satisfaction studies had been published. The Psychlit database of the American Psychological Association contained 3,690 entries from 1984 to June 24, 1996. With more than 300 published works per year, no one source could do more than sample this literature.

What this book has done is cover the major issues and topics that appear to be most important. By necessity, topics have been covered briefly, and in some cases, not at all. The serious student of this topic should consider this book as the initial introduction to the job satisfaction literature. Furthermore, most of what has been covered comes from the journals in industrial/organizational psychology and organizational behavior. Articles on job satisfaction can be found in the professional journals of most fields, including education, engineering, medicine, natural science, and social science. This is because this topic is of universal interest to working people, including those who conduct research and write journal articles.

Beyond the research literature and studies, job satisfaction is important in everyday life. Organizations have tremendous effects on the people who work in them. Some of those effects, as this book has shown, are reflected in how people feel about work. Negative feelings can lead to behaviors that are detrimental to organizations and potentially to adverse physical and psychological health. It is certainly within everyone's best interest for our organizations to function efficiently and smoothly. Organizational practices that maximize job satisfaction will likely have employees who are more cooperative and willing to help the organization be successful. It is also important that people maintain good health and positive well-being. Organizations can do much to help in this area by doing things to enhance job satisfaction.

Job satisfaction is an attitudinal variable that can be a diagnostic indicator of how a person is doing in one of the major domains of his or her life. Job dissatisfaction suggests that a problem exists either in the job or the person. As discussed in Chapter 4, many organizational conditions can lead to poor job attitudes. Also as discussed, sometimes events and factors outside of work can have negative effects on job satisfaction. These can include personal problems and personality of the individual. Job satisfaction on the other hand can be indicative of good work adjustment and positive well-being. Again both work and nonwork factors contribute to good job satisfaction.

Many organizations conduct periodic job satisfaction surveys of employees to diagnose problem areas that demand management attention. Areas of job dissatisfaction, either facets that are unusually low or places (e.g., work groups) that are lower than others, demand further investigation. Interventions designed to enhance job satisfaction can be tried. No one approach can be recommended as the problems are often idiosyncratic to each organization.

A potentially useful technique that many organizations have implemented to enhance job satisfaction is survey feedback. With this procedure, diagnostic activities are combined with targeted interventions designed specifically for the organization's specific problems. The first step is to conduct a job satisfaction survey of employees. The data are analyzed and placed into a report that is circulated to the employees who were surveyed. Usually, meetings of employees are held in which the findings are discussed. The purpose of the meetings is to develop an action plan to address the issues that were uncovered. Management then reviews the suggestions from the action plan and implements those seen as feasible.

Survey feedback has been demonstrated to be effective in enhancing the job satisfaction of participants (Bowers, 1973; Neuman, Edwards, & Raju, 1989). Of course, it is not the only intervention that has been used successfully. Pasmore, Francis, Haldeman, and Shani (1982) reviewed the outcomes of 134 studies in which one or more principles of sociotechnical systems theory (Trist & Bamforth, 1951) were applied in the workplace. These applications included autonomous work groups, feedback, increased responsibility, and rewards. Out of 54 studies in which job satisfaction was measured, 94% had positive effects. Although it is not always clear that the implemented changes were the cause of the attitude enhancement as Hawthorne effects cannot be ruled out in many of these sorts of studies, it seems likely that job satisfaction can be positively affected through organizational interventions.

Although the diagnosis of organizational problems through job satisfaction surveys can be beneficial, they can also cause considerable damage if done improperly. One should be careful about undertaking diagnostic activities without a commitment to make positive changes. The job satisfaction survey itself can raise expectations that management is concerned about employees. Lack of positive action following a survey is extremely frustrating to those who took the time to share concerns about the organization. Unfulfilled expectations can result in additional problems, such as counterproductive behavior and turnover. At the very least, there should be discussions throughout the organization about what can and cannot be done following a survey. Employees need to understand why dissatisfying situations must exist. Note that, sometimes, reasonable explanations can have very positive effects on behavior (e.g., Greenberg, 1990).

On the other hand, a properly conducted job satisfaction survey, when followed by reasonable interventions, is an activity that can have tremendous payoffs. When employees are offered the opportunity to participate in decisions that affect them, positive benefits can accrue to both organizations and people. Recent changes in the workplace, including reductions in supervisory personnel to monitor employees after downsizing (Kozlowski, Chao, Smith, & Hedlund, 1993) and rapid technological change, make each employee even more important to organizational survival than has been true in the past. As each employee is asked to contribute more because they have fewer coworkers to help with more difficult tasks, job satisfaction will become even more important for both individuals and organizations. In addition, organizations have the moral responsibility to treat employees well. Both moral and practical issues make job satisfaction a central concern of organizations and those who study them.

Appendix: The Job Satisfaction Survey

N ote: The purchaser of this book is given license to use and modify the Job Satisfaction Survey (JSS) for noncommercial academic and research purposes. This license does not allow the purchaser to sell the JSS alone or as part of a consulting package.

JOB SATISFACTION SURVEY
Paul E. Spector
Department of Psychology
University of South Florida

PLEASE CIRCLE THE ONE NUMBER FOR EACH QUESTION THAT COMES CLOSEST TO REFLECTING YOUR OPINION ABOUT IT.

		Disagree Very Much	Disagree Moderately	Disagree Slightly	Agree Slightly	Agree Moderately	Agree Very Much
1	I feel I am being paid a fair amount for the work I do.	1	2	3	4	5	6
2	There is really too little chance for promotion on my job.	1	2	3	4	5	6
3	My supervisor is quite competent in doing his/her job.	1	2	3	4	5	6
4	I am not satisfied with the benefits I receive.	1	2	3	4	5	6
5	When I do a good job, I receive the recognition for it that I should receive.	1	2	3	4	5	6
6	Many of our rules and procedures make doing a good job difficult.	1	2	3	4	5	6
7	I like the people I work with.	1	2	3	4	5	6
8	I sometimes feel my job is meaningless.	1	2	3	4	5	6
9	Communications seem good within this organization.	1	2	3	4	5	6
10	Raises are too few and far between.	1	2	3	4	5	6
11	Those who do well on the job stand a fair chance of being promoted.	1	2	3	4	5	6
12	My supervisor is unfair to me.	1	2	3	4	5	6
13	The benefits we receive are as good as most other organizations offer.	1	2	3	4	5	6
14	I do not feel that the work I do is appreciated.	1	2	3	4	5	6
15	My efforts to do a good job are seldom blocked by red tape.	1	2	3	4	5	6
16	I find I have to work harder at my job because of the incompetence of people I work with.	1	2	3	4	5	6
17	I like doing the things I do at work.	1	2	3	4	5	6
18	The goals of this organization are not clear to me.	1	2	3	4	5	6

(continued)

	PLEASE CIRCLE THE ONE NUMBER FOR EACH QUESTION THAT COMES CLOSEST TO REFLECTING YOUR OPINION ABOUT IT.	Disagree Very Much	Disagree Moderately	Disagree Slightly	Agree Slightly	Agree Moderately	Agree Very Much
19	I feel unappreciated by the organization when I think about what they pay me.	1	2	3	4	5	6
20	People get ahead as fast here as they do in other places.	1	2	3	4	5	6
21	My supervisor shows too little interest in the feelings of subordinates.	1	2	3	4	5	6
22	The benefit package we have is equitable.	1	2	3	4	5	6
23	There are few rewards for those who work here.	1	2	3	4	5	6
24	I have too much to do at work.	1	2	3	4	5	6
25	I enjoy my coworkers.	1	2	3	4	5	6
26	I often feel that I do not know what is going on with the organization.	1	2	3	4	5	6
27	I feel a sense of pride in doing my job.	1	2	3	4	5	6
28	I feel satisfied with my chances for salary increases.	1	2	3	4	5	6
29	There are benefits we do not have which we should have.	1	2	3	4	5	6
30	I like my supervisor.	1	2	3	4	5	6
31	I have too much paperwork.	1	2	3	4	5	6
32	I don't feel my efforts are rewarded the way they should be.	1	2	3	4	5	6
33	I am satisfied with my chances for promotion.	1	2	3	4	5	6
34	There is too much bickering and fighting at work.	1	2	3	4	5	6
35	My job is enjoyable.	1	2	3	4	5	6
36	Work assignments are not fully explained.	1	2	3	4	5	6

References

Akerstedt, T., & Theorell, T. (1976). Exposure to night work: Serum gastrin reactions, psychosomatic complaints and personality variables. *Journal of Psychosomatic Research, 20,* 479-484.

Arvey, R. D., Bouchard, T. J., Segal, N. L., & Abraham, L. M. (1989). Job satisfaction: Environmental and genetic components. *Journal of Applied Psychology, 74,* 187-192.

Arvey, R. D., & Dewhirst, H. D. (1979). Relationships between diversity of interests, age, job satisfaction and job performance. *Journal of Occupational Psychology, 52,* 17-23.

Arvey, R. D., Dewhirst, H. D., & Brown, E. M. (1978). A longitudinal study of the impact of changes in goal setting on employee satisfaction. *Personnel Psychology, 31,* 595-608.

Bacharach, S. B., Bamberger, P., & Conley, S. (1991). Work-home conflict among nurses and engineers: Mediating the impact of role stress on burnout and satisfaction at work. *Journal of Organizational Behavior, 12,* 39-53.

Balzer, W. K., Smith, P. C., Kravitz, D. E., Lovell, S. E., Paul, K. B., Reilly, B. A., & Reilly, C. E. (1990). *User's manual for the Job Descriptive Index (JDI) and the Job in General (JIG) scales.* Bowling Green, OH: Bowling Green State University.

Barling, J., & Gallagher, D. G. (1996). Part-time employment. In C. L. Cooper & I. T. Robertson (Eds.), *International review of industrial and organizational psychology, 1996* (pp. 243-277). Chichester, UK: Wiley.

Barling, J., & MacEwen, K. E. (1988). A multitrait-multimethod analysis of four maternal employment role experiences. *Journal of Organizational Behavior, 9,* 335-344.

Barton, J., & Folkard, S. (1991). The response of day and night nurses to their work schedules. *Journal of Occupational Psychology, 64,* 207-218.

Beatty, C. A. (1996). The stress of managerial and professional women: Is the price too high? *Journal of Organizational Behavior, 17,* 233-251.

Becker, T. E., & Billings, R. S. (1993). Profiles in commitment: An empirical test. *Journal of Organizational Behavior, 14,* 177-190.

Bedeian, A. G., Burke, B. G., & Moffett, R. G. (1988). Outcomes of work-family conflict among married male and female professionals. *Journal of Management, 14,* 475-491.

Bedeian, A. G., Ferris, G. R., & Kacmar, K. M. (1992). Age, tenure, and job satisfaction: A tale of two perspectives. *Journal of Vocational Behavior, 40,* 33-48.

Begley, T. M., & Czajka, J. M. (1993). Panel analysis of the moderating effects of commitment on job satisfaction, intent to quit, and health following organizational change. *Journal of Applied Psychology, 78,* 552-556.

Blau, G. (1993). Further exploring the relationship between job search and voluntary individual turnover. *Personnel Psychology, 46,* 313-330.

Bluedorn, A. C. (1982). A unified model of turnover from organizations. *Human Relations, 35,* 135-153.

Bluen, S. D., Barling, J., & Burns, W. (1990). Predicting sales performance, job satisfaction, and depression by using the achievement strivings and impatience-irritability dimensions of Type A behavior. *Journal of Applied Psychology, 75,* 212-216.

Bowers, D. G. (1973). OD techniques and their results in 23 organizations: The Michigan ICL study. *Journal of Applied Behavioral Science, 9,* 21-43.

Breaugh, J. A. (1983). The 12-hour work day: Differing employee reactions. *Personnel Psychology, 36,* 277-288.

Brief, A. P., Burke, M. J., George, J. M., Robinson, B., & Webster, J. (1988). Should negative affectivity remain an unmeasured variable in the study of job stress? *Journal of Applied Psychology, 73,* 193-198.

Brush, D. H., Moch, M. K., & Pooyan, A. (1987). Individual demographic differences and job satisfaction. *Journal of Occupational Behaviour, 8,* 139-155.

Buffum, W. E., & Konick, A. (1982). Employees' job satisfaction, residents' functioning, and treatment progress in psychiatric institutions. *Health & Social Work, 7,* 320-327.

Caldwell, D. F., & O'Reilly, C. A., III. (1990). Measuring person-job fit with a profile-comparison process. *Journal of Applied Psychology, 75,* 648-657.

Cammann, C., Fichman, M., Jenkins, D., & Klesh, J. (1979). *The Michigan Organizational Assessment Questionnaire.* Unpublished manuscript, University of Michigan, Ann Arbor.

Campion, M. A. (1988). Interdisciplinary approaches to job design: A constructive replication with extensions. *Journal of Applied Psychology, 73,* 467-481.

Campion, M. A. (1989). Ability requirement implications of job design: An interdisciplinary perspective. *Personnel Psychology, 42,* 1-24.

Campion, M. A., & McClelland, C. L. (1991). Interdisciplinary examination of the costs and benefits of enlarged jobs: A job design quasi-experiment. *Journal of Applied Psychology, 76,* 186-198.

Campion, M. A., & Thayer, P. W. (1985). Development and field evaluation of an interdisciplinary measure of job design. *Journal of Applied Psychology, 70,* 29-43.

Carsten, J. M., & Spector, P. E. (1987). Unemployment, job satisfaction, and employee turnover: A meta-analytic test of the Muchinsky model. *Journal of Applied Psychology, 72,* 374-381.

Chen, P. Y., & Spector, P. E. (1992). Relationships of work stressors with aggression, withdrawal, theft and substance use: An exploratory study. *Journal of Occupational and Organizational Psychology, 65,* 177-184.

Clark, A., Oswald, A., & Warr, P. (1996). Is job satisfaction U-shaped in age? *Journal of Occupational and Organizational Psychology, 69,* 57-81.

Cook, J. D., Hepworth, S. J., Wall, T. D., & Warr, P. B. (1981). *The experience of work.* New York: Academic Press.

Cooper, C. L., & Cartwright, S. (1994). Healthy mind; healthy organization: A proactive approach to occupational stress. *Human Relations, 47,* 455-471.

Cordes, C. L., & Dougherty, T. W. (1993). A review and an integration of research on job burnout. *Academy of Management Review, 18,* 621-656.

Crampton, S. M., & Wagner, J. A., III. (1994). Percept-percept inflation in microorganizational research: An investigation of prevalence and effect. *Journal of Applied Psychology, 79,* 67-76.

Cropanzano, R., James, K., & Konovsky, M. A. (1993). Dispositional affectivity as a predictor of work attitudes and job performance. *Journal of Organizational Behavior, 14,* 595-606.

Dalton, D. R., & Mesch, D. J. (1991). On the extent and reduction of avoidable absenteeism: An assessment of absence policy provisions. *Journal of Applied Psychology, 76,* 810-817.

Davis-Blake, A., & Pfeffer, J. (1989). Just a mirage: The search for dispositional effects in organizational research. *Academy of Management Review, 14,* 385-400.

DeVellis, R. F. (1991). *Scale development: Theory and applications.* Newbury Park, CA: Sage.

Dwyer, D. J., & Ganster, D. C. (1991). The effects of job demands and control on employee attendance and satisfaction. *Journal of Organizational Behavior, 12,* 595-608.

Eberhardt, B. J., & Shani, A. B. (1984). The effects of full-time versus part-time employment status on attitudes toward specific organizational characteristics and overall job satisfaction. *Academy of Management Journal, 27,* 893-900.

Edwards, J. R. (1991). Person-job fit: A conceptual integration, literature review, and methodological critique. In C. L. Cooper & I. T. Robertson (Eds.), *International review of industrial and organizational psychology, 1991* (pp. 283-357). Chichester, UK: Wiley.

Farh, J., Podsakoff, P. M., & Organ, D. W. (1990). Accounting for organizational citizenship behavior: Leader fairness and task scope versus satisfaction. *Journal of Management, 16,* 705-721.

Farrell, D., & Stamm, C. L. (1988). Meta-analysis of the correlates of employee absence. *Human Relations, 41,* 211-227.

Feldman, D. C. (1990). Reconceptualizing the nature and consequences of part-time work. *Academy of Management Review, 15,* 103-112.

Fletcher, B. C., & Jones, F. (1993). A refutation of Karasek's demand-discretion model of occupational stress with a range of dependent measures. *Journal of Organizational Behavior, 14,* 319-330.

Fox, M. L., Dwyer, D. J., & Ganster, D. C. (1993). Effects of stressful job demands and control on physiological and attitudinal outcomes in a hospital setting. *Academy of Management Journal, 36,* 289-318.

Frankenhaeuser, M., & Johansson, G. (1986). Stress at work: Psychobiological and psychosocial aspects. *International Review of Applied Psychology, 35,* 287-299.

Frese, M., & Zapf, D. (1988). Methodological issues in the study of work stress: Objective vs. subjective measurement of work stress and the question of longitudinal studies. In C. L. Cooper & R. Payne (Eds.), *Causes, coping and consequences of stress at work* (pp. 375-409). Chichester, UK: Wiley.

Fried, Y. (1991). Meta-analytic comparison of the Job Diagnostic Survey and Job Characteristics Inventory as correlates of work satisfaction and performance. *Journal of Applied Psychology, 76,* 690-697.

Fried, Y., & Ferris, G. R. (1987). The validity of the job characteristics model: A review and meta-analysis. *Personnel Psychology, 40,* 287-322.

Gallup Organization. (1995, June). People throughout the world largely satisfied with personal lives. *Gallup Organization International Newsletter.*

Ganster, D. C. (1980). Individual differences and task design: A laboratory experiment. *Organizational Behavior and Human Performance, 26,* 131-148.

Gerhart, B. (1987). How important are dispositional factors as determinants of job satisfaction? Implications for job design and other personnel programs. *Journal of Applied Psychology, 72,* 366-373.

Gerhart, B. (1990). Voluntary turnover and alternative job opportunities. *Journal of Applied Psychology, 5,* 467-476.

Gillet, B., & Schwab, D. P. (1975). Convergent and discriminant validities of corresponding Job Descriptive Index and Minnesota Satisfaction Questionnaire scales. *Journal of Applied Psychology, 60,* 313-317.

Glick, W. H., Jenkins, G. D., Jr., & Gupta, N. (1986). Method versus substance: How strong are underlying relationships between job characteristics and attitudinal outcomes? *Academy of Management Journal, 29,* 441-464.

Goff, S. J., Mount, M. K., & Jamison R. L. (1990). Employer supported child care, work/family conflict, and absenteeism: A field study. *Personnel Psychology, 43,* 794-809.

Greenberg, J. (1990). Employee theft as a reaction to underpayment inequity: The hidden cost of pay cuts. *Journal of Applied Psychology, 5,* 561-568.

Greenhaus, J. H., Parasuraman, S., & Wormley, W. M. (1990). Effects of race on organizational experiences, job performance evaluations, and career outcomes. *Academy of Management Journal, 33,* 64-86.

Griffeth, R. W. (1985). Moderation of the effects of job enrichment by participation: A longitudinal field experiment. *Organizational Behavior and Human Decision Processes, 35,* 73-93.

Griffeth, R. W., & Hom, P. W. (1987). Some multivariate comparisons of multinational managers. *Multivariate Behavioral Research, 22,* 173-191.

Griffin, R. W. (1991). Effects of work redesign on employee perceptions, attitudes, and behaviors: A long-term investigation. *Academy of Management Journal, 34,* 425-435.

Gupta, N., Jenkins, Jr., G. D., & Beehr, T. A. (1992). The effects of turnover on perceived job quality. *Group & Organization Management, 17,* 431-445.

Haccoun, R. R., & Jeanrie, C. (1995). Self reports of work absence as a function of personal attitudes toward absence, and perceptions of the organisation. *Applied Psychology: An International Review, 44,* 155-170.

Hackett, R. D., & Guion, R. M. (1985). A reevaluation of the absenteeism—job satisfaction relationship. *Organizational Behavior and Human Decision Processes, 35,* 340-381.

Hackman, J. R., & Oldham, G. R. (1974). *The Job Diagnostic Survey: An instrument for the diagnosis of jobs and the evaluation of job redesign projects* (Tech. Rep. No. 4). New Haven, CT: Yale University.

Hackman, J. R., & Oldham, G. R. (1975). Development of the Job Diagnostic Survey. *Journal of Applied Psychology, 60,* 159-170.

Hackman, J. R., & Oldham, G. R. (1976). Motivation through the design of work: Test of a theory. *Organizational Behavior and Human Performance, 16,* 250-279.

Hackman, J. R., & Oldham, G. R. (1980). *Work redesign.* Reading, MA: Addison-Wesley.

Hall, J. K. (1990). *Locus of control as a moderator of the relationship between perceived role ambiguity and reported work strains.* Unpublished doctoral dissertation, University of South Florida, Tampa.

Hammer, T. H., & Landau, J. (1981). Methodological issues in the use of absence data. *Journal of Applied Psychology, 66,* 574-581.

Harrison, D. A., & Shaffer, M. A. (1993, August). *Wading through Lake Woebegone: Comparative examinations of self reports and perceived norms of absenteeism.* Paper presented at Academy of Management Convention, Atlanta, GA.

Herzberg, F. (1968). One more time: How do you motivate employees? *Harvard Business Review,* January-February.

Herzberg, F., Mausner, B., & Snyderman, B. (1959). *The motivation to work.* New York: John Wiley.

Holahan, C., & Gilbert, L. (1979). Interrole conflict for working women: Careers versus jobs. *Journal of Applied Psychology, 64,* 86-90.

Hugick, L., & Leonard, J. (1991). Job dissatisfaction grows; "moonlighting" on the rise. *Gallup Poll News Service, 56,* 1-11.

Hulin, C. L., & Blood, M. R. (1968). Job enlargement, individual differences, and worker responses. *Psychological Bulletin, 69,* 41-55.

Hulin, C. L., Roznowski, M., & Hachiya, D. (1985). Alternative opportunities and withdrawal decisions: Empirical and theoretical discrepancies and an integration. *Psychological Bulletin, 97,* 233-250.

Iaffaldano, M. T., & Muchinsky, P. M. (1985). Job satisfaction and job performance: A meta-analysis. *Psychological Bulletin, 97,* 251-273.

Ironson, G. H., Smith, P. C., Brannick, M. T., Gibson, W. M., & Paul, K. B. (1989). Constitution of a Job in General Scale: A comparison of global, composite, and specific measures. *Journal of Applied Psychology, 74,* 193-200.

Jackofsky, E. F., & Peters, L. H. (1987). Part-time versus full-time employment status differences: A replication and extension. *Journal of Occupational Behaviour, 8,* 1-9.

Jackson, S. E., & Schuler, R. S. (1985). A meta-analysis and conceptual critique of research on role ambiguity and role conflict in work settings. *Organizational Behavior and Human Decision Processes, 36,* 16-78.

Jacobs, R., & Solomon, T. (1977). Strategies for enhancing the prediction of job performance from job satisfaction. *Journal of Applied Psychology, 62,* 417-421.

Jamal, M. (1990). Relationship of job stress and type-A behavior to employees' job satisfaction, organizational commitment, psychosomatic health problems, and turnover motivation. *Human Relations, 43,* 727-738.

Jamal, M., & Baba, V. V. (1992). Shiftwork and department-type related to job stress, work attitudes and behavioral intentions: A study of nurses. *Journal of Organizational Behavior, 13,* 449-464.

Jex, S. M., & Beehr, T. A. (1991). Emerging theoretical and methodological issues in the study of work-related stress. *Research in Personnel and Human Resources Management, 9,* 311-365.

Jex, S. M., & Gudanowski, D. M. (1992). Efficacy beliefs and work stress: An exploratory study. *Journal of Organizational Behavior, 13,* 509-517.

Johansson, G. (1981). Psychoneuroendocrine correlates of unpaced and paced performance. In G. Salvendy & M. J. Smith (Eds.), *Machine pacing and occupational stress.* London: Taylor & Francis.

Judge, T. A. (1992). The dispositional perspective in human resources research. *Research Personnel and Human Resources Management, 10,* 31-72.

Judge, T. A. (1993). Does affective disposition moderate the relationship between job satisfaction and voluntary turnover? *Journal of Applied Psychology, 78,* 395-401.

Judge, T. A., Boudreau, J. W., & Bretz, R. D., Jr. (1993). *Job and life attitudes of executives* (Working Paper No. 93-13). Ithaca, NY: Cornell University.

Judge, T. A., & Watanabe, S. (1993). Another look at the job satisfaction-life satisfaction relationship. *Journal of Applied Psychology, 78,* 939-948.

Karasek, R. A., Jr. (1979). Job demands, job decision latitude, and mental strain: Implications for job redesign. *Administrative Science Quarterly, 24,* 285-307.

Karasek, R. A., Jr., Gardell, B., & Lindell, J. (1987). Work and non-work correlates of illness and behaviour in male and female Swedish white collar workers. *Journal of Occupational Behaviour, 8,* 187-207.

Katz, D., & Kahn, R. L. (1978). *The social psychology of organizations* (2nd ed.). New York: John Wiley.

Keenan, A., & Newton, T. J. (1984). Frustration in organizations: Relationships to role stress, climate, and psychological strain. *Journal of Occupational Psychology, 57,* 57-65.

Kim, J. S. (1980). Relationships of personality to perceptual and behavioral responses in stimulating and nonstimulating tasks. *Academy of Management Journal, 23,* 307-318.

Kohler, S. S., & Mathieu, J. E. (1993). Individual characteristics, work perceptions, and affective reactions influences on differentiated absence criteria. *Journal of Organizational Behavior, 14,* 515-530.

Koller, M., Kundi, M., & Cervinka, R. (1978). Field studies of shift work at an Austrian oil refinery I: Health and psychosocial well-being of workers who drop out of shiftwork. *Ergonomics, 21,* 835-847.

Kozlowski, S. W. J., Chao, G. T., Smith, E. M., & Hedlund, J. (1993). Organizational downsizing: Strategies, interventions, and research implications. In C. L. Cooper & I. T. Robertson (Eds.), *International review of industrial and organizational psychology, 1993* (pp. 263-332). Chichester, UK: Wiley.

Krausz, M., & Freibach, N. (1983). Effects of flexible working time for employed women upon satisfaction, strains, and absenteeism. *Journal of Occupational Psychology, 56,* 155-159.

Kristof, A. L. (1996). Person-organization fit: An integrative review of its conceptualizations, measurement, and implications. *Personnel Psychology, 49,* 1-49.

Lammond, D. (1995). Unpublished data set. Macquarie University, Australia.

Lance, C. E., Lautenschlager, G. J., Sloan, C. E., & Varca, P. E. (1989). *Journal of Personality, 57,* 601-624.

Lawler, E. E., III, Hackman, J. R., & Kaufman, S. (1973). Effects of job redesign: A field experiment. *Journal of Applied Psychology, 58,* 49-62.

Lee, C., Ashford, S. J., & Bobko, P. (1990). Interactive effects of "Type A" behavior, and perceived control on worker performance, job satisfaction, and somatic complaints. *Academy of Management Journal, 33,* 870-881.

Lee, R. T., & Ashforth, B. E. (1993). A further examination of managerial burnout: Toward an integrated model. *Journal of Organizational Behavior, 14,* 3-20.

Lewis, S. N., & Cooper, C. L. (1987). Stress in two-earner couples and stage in the life-cycle. *Journal of Occupational Psychology, 60,* 289-303.

Lincoln, J. R., Hanada, M., & Olson, J. (1981). Cultural orientations and individual reactions to organizations: A study of employees of Japanese-owned firms. *Administrative Science Quarterly, 26,* 93-115.

Locke, E. A. (1976). The nature and causes of job satisfaction. In M. D. Dunnette (Ed.), *Handbook of industrial and organizational psychology* (pp. 1297-1349). Chicago: Rand McNally.

Loher, B. T., Noe, R. A., Moeller, N. L., & Fitzgerald, M. P. (1985). A meta-analysis of the relation of job characteristics to job satisfaction. *Journal of Applied Psychology, 70,* 280-289.

MacKenzie, S. B., Podsakoff, P. M., & Fetter, R. (1991). Organizational citizenship behavior and objective productivity as determinants of managerial evaluations of salespersons' performance. *Organizational Behavior and Human Decision Processes, 50,* 123-150.

Marion-Landais, C. A. (1993). *A cross-cultural study of leader-member exchange quality and job satisfaction as correlates of intra-dyadic work-value congruence.* Unpublished master's thesis, University of South Florida, Tampa.

Martocchio, J. J. (1994). The effects of absence culture on individual absence. *Human Relations, 47,* 243-262.

Maslach, C., & Jackson, S. (1981). *The Maslach Burnout Inventory.* Palo Alto, CA: Consulting Psychologists.

Mathieu, J. E., & Kohler, S. S. (1990). A cross-level examination of group absence influences on individual absence. *Journal of Applied Psychology, 75,* 217-220.

McNeely, B. L., & Meglino, B. M. (1994). The role of dispositional and situational antecedents in prosocial organizational behavior: An examination of the intended beneficiaries of prosocial behavior. *Journal of Applied Psychology, 79,* 836-844.

Melamed, S., Ben-Avi, I., Luz, J., & Green, M. S. (1995). Objective and subjective work monotony: Effects on job satisfaction, psychological distress, and absenteeism in blue-collar workers. *Journal of Applied Psychology, 80,* 29-42.

Miller, H. E., & Terborg, J. R. (1979). Job attitudes of part-time and full-time employees. *Journal of Applied Psychology, 64,* 380-386.

Mitra, A., Jenkins, G. D., Jr., & Gupta, N. (1992). A meta-analytic review of the relationship between absence and turnover. *Journal of Applied Psychology, 77,* 879-889.

Mobley, W. H., Griffeth, R. W., Hand, H. H., & Meglino, B. M. (1979). Review and conceptual analysis of the employee turnover process. *Psychological Bulletin, 86,* 493-522.

Moyle, P. (1995). The role of negative affectivity in the stress process: Tests of alternative models. *Journal of Organizational Behavior, 16,* 647-668.

Munene, J. C. (1995). "Not-on-seat": An investigation of some correlates of organisational citizenship behaviour in Nigeria. *Applied Psychology: An International Review, 44,* 111-122.

Neuman, G. A., Edwards, J. E., & Raju, N. S. (1989). Organizational development interventions: A meta-analysis of their effects on satisfaction and other attitudes. *Personnel Psychology, 42,* 461-483.

Newton, T., & Keenan, T. (1991). Further analyses of the dispositional argument in organizational behavior. *Journal of Applied Psychology, 76,* 781-787.

Nicholson, N., & Johns, G. (1985). The absence culture and the psychological contract: Who's in control of absence? *Academy of Management Review, 10,* 397-407.

Nunnally, J. C. (1978). *Psychometric theory* (2nd ed.). New York: McGraw-Hill.

O'Brien, G. E. (1983). Locus of control in work and retirement. In H. M. Lefcourt (Ed.), *Research in locus of control* (Vol. 3). New York: Academic Press.

O'Connor, E. J., Peters, L. H., Pooyan, A., Weekley, J., Frank, B., & Erenkrantz, B. (1984). Situational constraint effects on performance, affective reactions, and turnover: A field replication and extension. *Journal of Applied Psychology, 69,* 663-672.

O'Connor, E. J., Peters, L. H., Rudolf, C. J., & Pooyan, A. (1982). Situational constraints and employee affective reactions: A partial field replication. *Group & Organization Studies, 7,* 418-428.

O'Driscoll, M. P., & Beehr, T. A. (1994). Supervisor behaviors, role stressors and uncertainty as predictors of personal outcomes for subordinates. *Journal of Organizational Behavior, 15,* 141-155.

Organ, D. W., & Konovsky, M. (1989). Cognitive versus affective determinants of organizational citizenship behavior. *Journal of Applied Psychology, 74,* 157-164.

Organ, D. W., & Ryan, K. (1995). A meta-analytic review of attitudinal and dispositional predictors of organizational citizenship behavior. *Personnel Psychology, 48,* 775-802.

Orpen, C. (1979). The effects of job enrichment on employee satisfaction, motivation, involvement, and performance: A field experiment. *Human Relations, 32,* 189-217.

Palmore, E. (1969). Predicting longevity: A follow-up controlling for age. *The Gerontologist, 9,* 247-250.

Parasuraman, S., Greenhaus, J. H., & Granrose, C. S. (1992). Role stressors, social support, and well-being among two-career couples. *Journal of Organizational Behavior, 13,* 339-356.

Pasmore, W., Francis, C., Haldeman, J., & Shani, A. (1982). Sociotechnical systems: A North American reflection on empirical studies of the seventies. *Human Relations, 12,* 1179-1204.

Perlow, R., & Latham, L. L. (1993). Relationship of client abuse with locus of control and gender: A longitudinal study. *Journal of Applied Psychology, 78,* 831-834.

Peters, L. H., & O'Connor, E. J. (1980). Situational constraints and work outcomes: The influences of a frequently overlooked construct. *Academy of Management Review, 5,* 391-397.

Peters, L. H., O'Connor, E. J., & Rudolf, C. J. (1980). The behavioral and affective consequences of performance-relevant situational variables. *Organizational Behavior and Human Performance, 25,* 79-96.

Petty, M. M., McGee, G. W., & Cavender, J. W. (1984). A meta-analysis of the relationships between individual job satisfaction and individual performance. *Academy of Management Review, 9,* 712-721.

Pierce, J. L., & Dunham, R. B. (1992). The 12-hour work day: A 48-hour, eight-day week. *Academy of Management Journal, 35,* 1086-1098.

Pierce, J. L., & Newstrom, J. W. (1982). Employee responses to flexible work schedules: An inter-organization, inter-system comparison. *Journal of Management, 8,* 9-25.

Porter, L. W. (1962). Job attitudes in management: I. Perceived deficiencies in need fulfillment as a function of job level. *Journal of Applied Psychology, 46,* 375-384.

Raggatt, P. T. (1991). Work stress among long-distance coach drivers: A survey and correlational study. *Journal of Organizational Behavior, 12,* 565-579.

Rain, J. S., Lane I. M., & Steiner, D. D. (1991). A current look at the job satisfaction/life satisfaction relationship: Review and future considerations. *Human Relations, 44,* 287-305.

Ralston, D. A. (1989). The benefits of flextime: Real or imagined? *Journal of Organizational Behavior, 10,* 369-373.

Rice, R. W., Frone, M. R., & McFarlin, D. B. (1992). Work-nonwork conflict and the perceived quality of life. *Journal of Organizational Behavior, 13,* 155-168.

Rice, R. W., Phillips, S. M., & McFarlin, D. B. (1990). Multiple discrepancies and pay satisfaction. *Journal of Applied Psychology, 75,* 386-393.

Roberts, K. H., & Glick, W. (1981). The job characteristics approach to task design: A critical review. *Journal of Applied Psychology, 66,* 193-217.

Roethlisberger, F. J. (1941). *Management and morale.* Cambridge, MA: Harvard University Press.

Ronen, S., & Primps, S. B. (1981). The compressed work week as organizational change: Behavioral and attitudinal outcomes. *Academy of Management Review, 6,* 61-74.

Rotter, J. B. (1966). Generalized expectancies for internal versus external control of reinforcement. *Psychological Monographs, 80*(1), no. 609.

Roznowski, M. (1989). Examination of the measurement properties of the job descriptive index with experimental items. *Journal of Applied Psychology, 74,* 805-814.

Salancik, G. R., & Pfeffer, J. (1978). A social information processing approach to job attitudes and task design. *Administrative Science Quarterly, 23,* 224-253.

Sargent, L., & Terry, D. J. (1994, August). *The effects of work control and job demands on employee adjustment and work performance.* Paper presented at the Academy of Management Conference, Dallas.

Schaubroeck, J., Ganster, D. C., & Fox, M. L. (1992). Dispositional affect and work-related stress. *Journal of Applied Psychology, 77,* 322-335.

Schaubroeck, J., Ganster, D. C., & Kemmerer, B. E. (1994). Job complexity, "type A" behavior, and cardiovascular disorder: A prospective study. *Academy of Management Journal, 37,* 426-439.

Schmitt, N., Coyle, B. W., White, J. K., & Rauschenberger, J. (1978). Background, needs, job perceptions, and job satisfaction: A causal model. *Personnel Psychology, 31,* 889-901.

Schnake, M. (1991). Organizational citizenship: A review, proposed model, and research agenda. *Human Relations, 44,* 735-759.

Schneider, B., & Dachler, H. P. (1978). A note on the stability of the Job Descriptive Index. *Journal of Applied Psychology, 63,* 650-653.

Schriesheim, C. A., Powers, K. J., Scandura, T. A., Gardiner, C. C., & Landau, M. J. (1993). Improving construct measurement in management research: Comments and a quantitative approach for assessing the theoretical content adequacy of paper-and-pencil survey-type instruments. *Journal of Management, 19,* 385-417.

Scott, K. D., & Taylor, G. S. (1985). An examination of conflicting findings on the relationship between job satisfaction and absenteeism: A meta-analysis. *Academy of Management Journal, 28,* 599-612.

Shirom, A. (1989). Burnout in work organizations. In C. L. Cooper & I. T. Robertson (Eds.), *International review of industrial and organizational psychology, 1989* (pp. 25-48). Chichester, UK: Wiley.

Shore, L. M., Newton, L. A., & Thornton, G. C., III. (1990). Job and organizational attitudes in relation to employee behavioral intentions. *Journal of Organizational Behavior, 57,* 57-67.

Sims, H. P., Jr., Szilagyi, A. D., & Keller, R. T. (1976). The measurement of job characteristics. *Academy of Management Journal, 19,* 195-212.

Slocum, J. W., Jr., & Topichak, P. M. (1972). Do cultural differences affect job satisfaction? *Journal of Applied Psychology, 56,* 177-178.

Smith, C. A., Organ, D. W., & Near, P. J. (1983). Organizational citizenship behavior: Its nature and antecedents. *Journal of Applied Psychology, 68,* 653-663.

Smith, M. J., Hurrell, J. J., Jr., & Murphy, R. K., Jr. (1981). Stress and health effects in paced and unpaced work. In G. Salvendy & M. J. Smith (Eds.), *Machine pacing and occupational stress.* London: Taylor & Francis.

Smith, P. B., & Misumi, J. (1989). Japanese management: A sun rising in the West? In C. L. Cooper & I. T. Robertson (Eds.), *International review of industrial and organizational psychology, 1989* (pp. 329-369). Chichester, UK: Wiley.

Smith, P. C., Kendall, L. M., & Hulin, C. L. (1969). *Measurement of satisfaction in work and retirement.* Chicago: Rand McNally.

Spector, P. E. (1982). Behavior in organizations as a function of employees' locus of control. *Psychological Bulletin, 91,* 482-497.

Spector, P. E. (1985). Measurement of human service staff satisfaction: Development of the Job Satisfaction Survey. *American Journal of Community Psychology, 13,* 693-713.

Spector, P. E. (1986). Perceived control by employees: A meta-analysis of studies concerning autonomy and participation at work. *Human Relations, 11,* 1005-1016.

Spector, P. E. (1987). Interactive effects of perceived control and job stressors on affective reactions and health outcomes for clerical workers. *Work & Stress, 1,* 155-162.

Spector, P. E. (1988). Development of the Work Locus of Control Scale. *Journal of Occupational Psychology, 61,* 335-340.

Spector, P. E. (1992a). A consideration of the validity and meaning of self-report measures of job conditions. In C. L. Cooper & I. T. Robertson (Eds.), *International review of industrial and organizational psychology, 1992* (pp. 123-151). Chichester, UK: Wiley.

Spector, P. E. (1992b). *Summated Rating Scale construction: An introduction* (Sage University Paper series on Quantitative Applications in the Social Sciences, No. 07-082). Newbury Park, CA: Sage.

Spector, P. E. (1997). The role of frustration in anti-social behavior at work. In R. A. Giacalone & J. Greenberg (Eds.), *Anti-social behavior in the workplace* (pp. 1-17). Thousand Oaks, CA: Sage.

Spector, P. E., Dwyer, D. J., & Jex, S. M. (1988). Relation of job stressors to affective, health, and performance outcomes: A comparison of multiple data sources. *Journal of Applied Psychology, 73,* 11-19.

Spector, P. E., & Jex, S. M. (1991). Relations of job characteristics from multiple data sources with employee affect, absence, turnover intentions, and health. *Journal of Applied Psychology, 76,* 46-53.

Spector, P. E., & O'Connell, B. J. (1994). The contribution of personality traits, negative affectivity, locus of control and Type A to the subsequent reports of job stressors and job strains. *Journal of Occupational and Organizational Psychology, 67,* 1-11.

Spector, P. E., & Wimalasiri, J. (1986). A cross-cultural comparison of job satisfaction dimensions in the United States and Singapore. *International Review of Applied Psychology, 35,* 147-158.

Staw, B. M., Bell, N. E., & Clausen, J. A. (1986). The dispositional approach to job attitudes: A lifetime longitudinal test. *Administrative Science Quarterly, 31,* 56-77.

Staw, B. M., & Ross, J. (1985). Stability in the midst of change: A dispositional approach to job attitudes. *Journal of Applied Psychology, 70,* 469-480.

Steers, R. M., & Rhodes, S. (1978). Major influences on employee attendance: A process model. *Journal of Applied Psychology, 63,* 391-407.

Stewart, W., & Barling, J. (1996). Fathers' work experiences effect children's behaviors via job-related affect and parenting behaviors. *Journal of Organizational Behavior, 17,* 221-232.

Storms, P. L., & Spector, P. E. (1987). Relationships of organizational frustration with reported behavioural reactions: The moderating effect of locus of control. *Journal of Occupational Psychology, 60,* 227-234.

Taber, T. D., & Taylor, E. (1990). A review and evaluation of the psychometric properties of the Job Diagnostic Survey. *Personnel Psychology, 43,* 467-500.

Tett, R. P., & Meyer, J. P. (1993). Job satisfaction, organizational commitment, turnover intention, and turnover: Path analysis based on meta-analytic findings. *Personnel Psychology, 46,* 259-293.

Tharenou, P. (1993). A test of reciprocal causality for absenteeism. *Journal of Organizational Behavior, 14,* 269-290.

Thomas, L. T., & Ganster, D. C. (1995). Impact of family-supportive work variables on work-family conflict and strain: A control perspective. *Journal of Applied Psychology, 80,* 6-15.

Trice, A. D., & Tillapaugh, P. (1991). Children's estimates of their parents' job satisfaction. *Psychological Reports, 69,* 63-66.

Trist, E. L., & Bamforth, K. W. (1951). Some social and psychological consequences of the longwall method of coal-getting. *Human Relations, 4,* 3-38.

Tuch, S. A., & Martin, J. K. (1991). Race in the workplace: Black/white differences in the sources of job satisfaction. *Sociological Quarterly, 32,* 103-116.

Waddell, F. T. (1983). Factors affecting choice, satisfaction, and success in female self-employed. *Journal of Vocational Behavior, 23,* 292-304.

Wall, T. D., Corbett, J. M., Martin, R., Clegg, C. W., & Jackson, P. R. (1990). Advanced manufacturing technology, work design, and performance: A change study. *Journal of Applied Psychology, 75,* 691-697.

Wall, T. D., & Martin, R. (1987). Job and work design. In C. L. Cooper & I. T. Robertson (Eds.), *International review of industrial and organizational psychology, 1987* (pp. 61-92). Chichester, UK: Wiley.

Warr, P., & Payne, R. (1983). Affective outcomes of paid employment in a random sample of British workers. *Journal of Occupational Behaviour, 4,* 91-104.

Watson, D., Pennebaker, J. W., & Folger, R. (1986). Beyond negative affectivity: Measuring stress and satisfaction in the workplace. *Journal of Organizational Behavior Management, 8,* 141-157.

Weaver, C. N. (1978). Job satisfaction as a component of happiness among males and females. *Personnel Psychology, 31,* 831-840.

Weiss, D. J., Dawis, R. V., England, G. W., & Lofquist, L. H. (1967). *Manual for the Minnesota Satisfaction Questionnaire* (Minnesota Studies in Vocational Rehabilitation, No. 22). University of Minnesota, Minneapolis.

Weiss, D. J., Dawis, R. V., Lofquist, L. H., & England, G. W. (1966). *Instrumentation for the theory of work adjustment* (Minnesota Studies in Vocational Rehabilitation, No. 21). University of Minnesota, Minneapolis.

Weitz, J. (1952). A neglected concept in the study of job satisfaction. *Personnel Psychology, 5,* 201-205.

Westman, M. (1992). Moderating effect of decision latitude on stress-strain relationship: Does organizational level matter? *Journal of Organizational Behavior, 13,* 713-722.

Wexley, K. N., Alexander, R. A., Greenawalt, J. P., & Couch, M. A. (1980). Attitudinal congruence and similarity as related to interpersonal evaluations in manager-subordinate dyads. *Academy of Management Journal, 23,* 320-330.

White, A. T., & Spector, P. E. (1987). An investigation of age-related factors in the age-job satisfaction relationship. *Psychology and Aging, 2,* 261-265.

Williams, L. J., Gavin, M. B., & Williams, M. L. (1996). Measurement and nonmeasurement processes with negative affectivity and employee attitudes. *Journal of Applied Psychology, 81,* 88-101.

Witt, L. A., & Nye, L. G. (1992). Gender and the relationship between perceived fairness of pay or promotion and job satisfaction. *Journal of Applied Psychology, 77,* 910-917.

Wolf, M. G. (1970). Need gratification theory: A theoretical reformulation of job satisfaction/dissatisfaction and job motivation. *Journal of Applied Psychology, 54,* 87-94.

Wright, J. D., & Hamilton, R. F. (1978). Work satisfaction and age: Some evidence for the "job change" hypothesis. *Social Forces, 56,* 1140-1158.

Zeitz, G. (1990). Age and work satisfaction in a government agency: A situational perspective. *Human Relations, 43,* 419-438.

Zultowski, W. H., Arvey, R. D., & Dewhirst, H. D. (1978). Moderating effects of organizational climate on relationships between goal-setting attributes and employee satisfaction. *Journal of Vocational Behavior, 12,* 217-227.

Author Index

88

Subject Index

Absence, 59-62
Absence culture, 62
Accidents, 47
Age and job satisfaction, 25-26
Aggression, 67-68
Alcohol consumption, 47
Altruism, 57
American pattern of job satisfaction, 23-24, 26-27
Anxiety, 43, 66
Assessment procedures, 6
Autonomous work groups, 73
Autonomy, 31-34, 36, 43

Burnout, 65-66

Catecholamines, 67
Circadian rhythms, 48
Compensation hypothesis, 70
Compliance, 57
Control, 43-45, 68
Core characteristics, 31, 32
Counterproductive behavior, 67-68
Country differences in job satisfaction, 26-28

Critical incident technique, 38
Critical Psychological States, 31, 32
Cycle time, 37

Demand/Control Model, 45
Depersonalization, 66
Depression, 67
Digestive problems, 48
Downsizing, 73

Emotional exhaustion, 66
Existing scales, advantages of, 6
Existing scales, cost of, 6, 17
Extra-role conflict, 39
Extrinsic job satisfaction, 15

Facets, 2-4
Family friendly work policies, 41
Fatigue, 47
Flexible work schedules, 46
Frustration, 68

Gallup Polls, 7, 23-24, 40, 41, 69
Gender and job satisfaction, 25, 28

About the Author

Paul E. Spector is Professor of Industrial/Organizational Psychology at the University of South Florida. His research interests include both the content and methodology of the field. Content areas concern the impact of jobs on the behavior and well-being of employees, including counterproductive behavior, job satisfaction, job stress, and withdrawal behavior. Methodological areas are complex statistics and psychological measurement. Professor Spector has published in many journals of the field, including *Journal of Applied Psychology, Journal of Management, Journal of Organizational Behavior (JOB), Journal of Occupational and Organizational Psychology (JOOP),* and *Psychological Bulletin.* He has written three other books for Sage Publications on computer programming with the SAS language and research methodology. He also has written an industrial/ organizational psychology textbook. At present, he is an associate editor for *JOOP,* and the Point/Counterpoint editor for *JOB.* In addition to writing this book, he is a member of the editorial board for this **Advanced Topics in Organizational Behavior** book series.